EUROPE IN 22 DAYS

A Step by Step Guide and Travel Itinerary

by Rick Steves

maps by David C. Hoerlein
cover by Jennifer Dewey

Library of Congress Catalog Card No. 84-0433188
ISBN 0-912528-43-5

Published by John Muir Publications
Santa Fe, New Mexico

10 9 8 7 6 5 4 3 2

Distributed to the trade by W. W. Norton & Co.
New York, NY

Contents

How to Use This Book

This book is the tour guide in your pocket. It lets you be the boss by giving you the best basic 22 days in Europe and a suggested way to use each of those days most efficiently. It is for do-it-yourselfers — with or without a tour.

Europe in 22 Days originated (and is still used) as the tour handbook for those who join me on my "Back Door Europe" Tours. Since most large organized tours work to keep their masses ignorant while visiting many of the same places we'll cover, this book is vital to anyone who hopes to maintain independence and flexibility while taking a typical big bus tour.

Realistically, most travelers are interested in the predictable biggies — Rhine castles, Sistine Chapel, Eiffel Tower and beerhalls. This tour covers those while mixing in a good dose of "back door intimacy" with Italian hilltowns, forgotten Riviera ports and Swiss Alp villages.

While the trip is designed as a car tour (3000 miles), it also makes a great three-week train trip. Each day's journey is adapted for train travel with explanations, options and appropriate train schedules included.

A three-week car rental (split two ways) or a three-week first class Eurailpass costs $330 at this writing. It costs $600 to $800 to fly roundtrip to Amsterdam. For room and board figure $20 a day for 22 days, totalling $440. This is a feasible budget if you know the tricks — see *Europe Through the Back Door*. Add $200 or $300 fun money and you've got yourself a great European adventure for $1,800. Do it!

Of course, connect-the-dots travel isn't perfect, just as color-by-numbers ain't good art. But this book is your friendly Frenchman, your German in a jam, your handbook. It's your well-thought-out and tested itinerary. I've done it — and refined it — sixteen times on my own and with groups. Use it, take advantage of it, but don't let it rule you. Try to travel outside of peak season, anytime but June 20 through August 20, so finding hotels won't be a problem; wear a moneybelt; use local tourist information centers; and don't be an "Ugly American."

This book should be read through completely before your trip, and then used as a rack to hang more ideas on. As you study and travel and plan and talk to people you'll fill it with notes. It's your tool. The book is completely modular and is adaptable to any European trip. You'll find 22 units — or days — each built with the same sections:

1. **Introductory overview** for the day.
2. Sample day plan with: List of most important **Sightseeing Highlights** (rated: ***Don't miss; **Try hard to see; *Worthwhile if you can make it); an hourly **Suggested Schedule** that I use and recommend for that day; **Helpful Hints** on orientation, shopping, transportation, day-to-day chores.
3. **Food and Lodging:** How and where to find the best budget places, including addresses, phone numbers, and my favorites.
4. An easy-to-read **map** locating all recommended places.
5. **Transportation** plan for drivers, plus an adapted plan with schedules for train travelers.
6. **Optional itinerary** for those with more or less than the suggested time, or with particular interests. This itinerary is *rubbery!*

For each country there is also a **culture review** and **practical phrase list.** The back of the book includes post-trip options, several suggested regional 22-day trips, a climate chart and list of local festivals for 1985 and 1986, and more.

Tips

Efficient Travelers Think Ahead

This itinerary assumes you are a well-organized traveler who lays departure groundwork upon arrival, reads a day ahead in the itinerary book, keeps a list of all the things that should be taken care of, and avoids problems whenever possible before they happen.

When to Go

Peak season (July and August) is most difficult. During this very crowded time it's best to arrive early in the day and call hotels in advance (call from one hotel to the next; your receptionist can help you). Things like banking, laundry stops, good mail days and picnics should be anticipated and planned for. If you expect to travel smart, you will. If you insist on being confused, your trip will be a mess.

Prices

For simplicity I've priced things throughout this book in dollars. These prices, as well as the hours, telephone numbers and so on, are accurate as of November 1984. Things are always changing and I have tossed timidity out the window knowing you'll understand that this book, like any guidebook, starts growing old before it's even printed. Please don't expect Europe to have stood still entirely since this book was written, and do what you can to call ahead or double-check hours and times when you arrive.

How to Use This Book

Border Crossings

Passing from one country to another in Europe is generally extremely easy. Sometimes you won't even realize it's happened. When you do change countries, however, you change money, postage stamps, and much more. Plan ahead for these changes. (Coins and stamps are worthless outside of their home countries.)

Language & Culture

You will be dealing with an intensely diverse language and customs situation; work to adapt. In sheer bulk, the USA may be big but it's bound by common language. The countries of Europe are not. We just assume Germany is "Germany"; but Germany is "Tedesco" to the Italians, "Allemagne" to the French, and "Deutschland" to the people who live there. While we think shower curtains are logical, many countries just protect the toilet paper and let the rest of the room shower with you.

Scheduling

Your overall itinerary strategy is a fun challenge. Read through this book and note the problem days when most musuems are closed (i.e. Paris — Tuesday; Florence and Amsterdam — Monday). Sundays have the same pros and cons as they do for travelers in the USA. Saturdays in Europe are virtually week days. It's good to mix intense and relaxed periods. Every trip needs at least a few slack days.

Keeping Up with the News (If You Must)

To keep in touch with world and American news while traveling in Europe, I use the *International Herald Tribune* which comes out almost daily via satellite from many places in Europe. Every Tuesday the European editions of *Time* and *Newsweek* hit the stands. They are full of articles of particular interest to European travelers. Many British newspapers find their way to the continent, but most are nearly worthless (unless you're a *National Enquirer* fan).

Remember, news in English will only be sold where there's enough demand — in big cities and tourist centers.

Recommended Guidebooks

This small book is your itinerary handbook. To really enjoy and appreciate these busy three weeks, you'll also need some directory-type guidebook information. I know it hurts to spend $30 or $40 on extra guidebooks, but when you consider the improvements they will make in your $2000 vacation — not to mention the money they'll save you — *not* buying them would be perfectly "penny-wise and pound-foolish." Here is my recommended guidebook strategy.

1. **General low-budget directory-type guidebook** — You need one. *Let's Go: Europe* is the best. If its youthful approach is not yours, then Arthur Frommer's individual country guidebooks are next best (for Germany, France and Italy). Frommer's *Europe on $25 a Day* is helpful for only the big cities. For this trip, you can just rip out the chapters on Venice, Rome, Florence and Paris. If you like the *Let's Go* style, the individual books in that series (Italy and France) are the best anywhere.

2. **Cultural and sightseeing guides** — The tall green Michelin guides (Germany, Austria, Italy, Switzerland, Paris) have nothing about room and board but everything else you'll ever need to know about the sights, customs and culture. I found the new little blue American Express Guides to Venice, Florence, Rome and Paris even handier than the Michelin, but expensive.

3. **Phrase books** — Unless you speak German, Italian and French, you'd better cover your linguistic bases with a phrase book. Berlitz puts out great pocket guides to each of those languages as well as a little book with 14 European languages covered more briefly (but adequately for me). Berlitz also has a pocket-sized 14-language menu phrase book ideal for those galloping gluttons who plan to eat their way through Europe. *Frommer's Fast n' Easy Phrase Book* covering Europe's four major languages (German, Italian, French and Spanish) is new and ideal for our itinerary.

4. **Rick Steves' books** — Finally, I've written this book assuming you've read or will read the latest editions of my books *Europe Through the Back Door* and *Europe 101*.

   To keep this book small and pocket-sized, I have resisted the temptation to repeat the most applicable and important information already included in my other books; there is no overlap.

   Europe Through the Back Door gives you the basic skills, the foundation which makes this demanding 22-day plan possible. Chapters on: minimizing jet lag, packing light, driving or train travel, finding budget beds without reservations, changing money, theft and the tourist, hurdling the language barrier, health, travel photography, long-distance telephoning in Europe, travelers' toilet trauma, ugly-Americanism, laundry, and itinerary strategies and techniques that are so very important. The book also includes special articles on 32 "Back Doors," eight of which are included in this tour (Hilltowns, Civita, Cinqueterre, Romantic Road, Castle Day, Swiss Alps, Alsace and Versailles).

   Europe 101 gives you the story of Europe's people, history and art. Your bookstore should have these two books (available through John Muir Publications), or you can order directly (see page 104).

How to Use This Book

Books I would buy for this trip: (1) *Let's Go: Europe* (rip out appropriate chapters) $9.95, (2) *Europe on $25 a Day* (take only applicable chapters) $10.95, (3) *Frommer's Fast n' Easy Phrase Book,* $6.95, (4) *Michelin's Green Guide* for Italy, $9.95. That comes to $38, or $19 each for two people.

And, of course, I'd read *Europe Through the Back Door* and *Europe 101* at home before departing. Of all the books mentioned, only the Michelin guides are available in Europe; better yet, they are available in English and are cheaper than in the USA.

My goal is to free you, not chain you. Please defend your spontaneity like you would your mother, and use this book to avoid time- and money-wasting mistakes, to get more intimate with Europe by traveling as a temporary local person, and as a point of departure from which to shape your best possible travel experience.

Anyone who has read this far has what it takes intellectually to do this tour independently. Be confident, enjoy the hills and the valleys, and *Bon voyage!*

Back Door Travel Philosophy
as taught in Europe Through the Back Door

TRAVEL IS INTENSIFIED LIVING — maximum thrills per minute and one of the last great sources of legal adventure. In many ways, the less you spend the more you get.

Experiencing the real thing requires candid informality — going "Through the Back Door."

Traditional travel writing gives its readers an eloquent void — a thousand column inches wide. Rick Steve's books will fill that hole, preparing and encouraging you to experience the world— from Walla Walla to Bora Bora.

We'll discuss problems and offer solutions, bolstered by cocky optimism. Too much travel writing comes from free trips. A guest of a country's tourist industry gains experience helpful only to other guests of the industry. We travel the way you will, making mistakes so you can learn from them. Our intent is to expose, enthuse, educate — then entertain. We'll dispel myths and conquer fears and apprehensions that inhibit travelers. We'll widen your comfort zone. Here are a few of our beliefs:

Affording travel is a matter of priorities. Many people who "can't afford a trip" could sell their car and travel for two years.

You can travel anywhere in the world for $20 a day plus transportation costs. Money has little to do with enjoying your trip. In fact, spending more money builds a thicker wall between you and what you came to see.

A tight budget forces you to travel "close to the ground," meeting and communicating with the people, not relying on service with a purchased smile. Never sacrifice sleep, nutrition, safety or cleanliness in the name of budget. Simply enjoy the local-style alternatives to expensive hotels and restaurants.

Extroverts have more fun. If your trip is low on magic moments, kick yourself and start making things happen. Dignity and good travel don't mix.

If you don't enjoy a place it's often because you don't know enough about it. Seek out the truth. Recognize tourist traps.

A culture is legitimized by its existence. Give a people the benefit of your open mind. Think of things as different but not better or worse.

Back Door Travel Philosophy

Of course, travel, like the world, is a series of hills and valleys. Be fanatically positive and militantly optimistic.

Travel is addicting. It can make you a happier American, as well as a citizen of the world. Our Earth is home to five billion equally important people. That's wonderfully humbling.

Globetrotting destroys ethno-centricity and encourages the understanding and appreciation of various cultures. Travel changes people. Many travelers toss aside their "hometown blinders," assimilating the best points of different cultures into their own character.

The world is a cultural garden. We're working on the ultimate salad. Won't you join us?

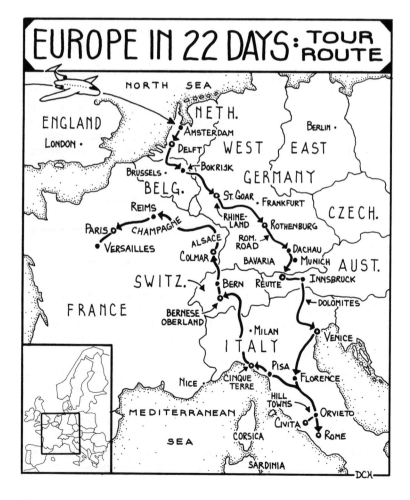

Itinerary

DAY

1   Depart

2   Arrive at Amsterdam's Schipol Airport (always the next day). Pick up car or activate Eurailpass. Drive to Delft, or a small town outside of Amsterdam, check into hotel.

3   (All breakfasts are served in hotel at about 7:30 or 8:00.) One hour drive to Amsterdam. Orientation tour, visit Anne Frank's house, 3 hours to tour Van Gogh and Rijksmuseum, picnic lunch in park, 1 hour canal tour, 1 Hour free to explore or shop. Return to Delft for Indonesian feast, "Rice Table." Evening free in very typical Dutch town.

4   Drive to Belgian open-air folk museum at Bokrijk, largest and best in Low Countries. With local guided folk life tour. Picnic lunch. Drive into Germany. Check into a gasthaus on the Rhine. Dinner below a castle.

5   Tour largest castle on Rhine, Rhinefells. Cruise from St. Goar to Bacharach past most famous castles on Rhine. Picnic in park at Bacharach with free time in town. Drive via autobahn to Rothenburg. Dinner in gasthaus within medieval town walls.

6   Pre-breakfast walk around city wall. Morning introductory tour. Rest of day free for sightseeing or shopping. Best shopping town in Germany. Dinner at gasthaus. Evening is best spent in a winestube or beerhall.

7   Morning, explore the Romantic Road, Germany's medieval heartland. Picnic lunch. Afternoon tour of Dachau concentration camp. Dinner and evening in Tirolian town of Reutte. Dinner at gasthaus.

8   "Castle Day" today. Beat the crowds to Mad King Ludwig's magnificent Neuschwanstein Castle. Visit the best example of Bavarian Baroque-Rococo style church architecture, the Weiss Church. Time to explore busy Oberammergau before returning to our Austrian homebase to climb to the ruined castles of Ehrenburg. Dinner at our gasthaus. Evening free to find some Tirolean fun.

9   Morning free in Innsbruck's historic center with time to enjoy its great Tirolean folk museum. Picnic at the Olympic ski jump, then a wondrous Alpine drive into sunny Italy. Evening cruise down Venice's Grand Canal, orientation tour and check into our very central hotel "Citta di Berna." After a typical Venetian dinner enjoy Gelati, cappuchino, and the magical atmosphere of St. Mark's at night!

Itinerary

10   Morning tour of highlights of Venice — Doge's Palace, St. Mark's, Campanile. Rest of day free. Evening, famous "Back Door Venetian Pub Crawl Dinner."

11   Leave very early for three hour drive to Florence. All day in Europe's art capital with tour covering David, Duomo and other highlights. Free time for shopping or more museums. Evening drive into Rome.

12   Walk through classical Rome — Colosseum, Forum, Capitol Hill. Lunch and siesta at hotel or convent. Afternoon visit Pantheon, then on to St. Peter's to visit Europe's greatest cathedral. Time to climb the 300-foot high dome for great city view. Dinner in colorful Trastevere district. Evening walk through Trastevere, over the Tiber River and on to Piazza Navona for Turtufo ice cream, people-watching and the floodlit Trevi Fountain.

13   Morning free to shop or sightsee or snooze. Afternoon to enjoy the Vatican Museum and Michaelangelo's Sistine Chapel. Evening drive north to Bagnareggio near Orvieto to the hilltown craziness of Angelino, a great feast, homemade wine, a possible "in-house disco" and a trip in to "La Cantina" — memorable, to say the least.

14   All day to explore hilltowns. Morning visit to cute little Civita. Lunch in its only piazza. Afternoon to explore an Etruscan tomb (500 B.C.) and the famous hilltown of Orvieto. Evening back at Angelino's for dinner and more Italian fun.

15   Drive north to Cinqueterre. Lunch and time to climb the tower at Pisa. Afternoon leave bus in La Spezia and take train into the Italian Riviera. Vernazza is our headquarters village for this vacation from our vacation. Fresh seafood and local wine at Sr. Sorisso's Pension — the only place to stay in this traffic-free town. Evening is yours — romance guaranteed on the breakwater.

16   All day free for hiking, exploring villages, swimming, relaxing on the beach. Fun in the sun. You'll fall in love with the Italian Riviera. Dinner at Sorriso's. Evening free.

17   Leave very early. Drive along Riviera to Genoa, then north past Milan into Switzerland. After a stop in Italian Switzerland, Ticino, we climb over Susten Pass and into the heart of the Swiss Alps, the Bernese Oberland. After a stop in Interlaken, we'll ride the gondola to the stop just before heaven, Gimmelwald. This traffic-free alpine fairytale village has only one chalet-hotel, Hotel Mittaghorn, and that's where we'll stay. Walter will have a hearty dinner waiting.

18   Today is hike day. We'll spend the day very memorably above the clouds in the region of the Jungfrau and the Eiger. Dinner with fondue at Walter's. Evening massage, coffee-schnapps and Swiss chocolate party.

19   Free day. Optional lift up to the 10,000-foot Schilthorn for breakfast and hike down. Or sit in a meadow and be Heidi. Or shop and explore through one of the villages of Lauterbrunnen Valley. Early dinner at Walter's (he's every Back Door tour's favorite cook) before driving out of Switzerland and into France. Evening in Colmar, Alsace where we'll check into the Hotel Rapp.

20   All day to explore historic Colmar and the Wine Road (Route du Vin) of the Alsace region. Lovely villages, wine tasting and tours, and some powerful art. Evening free in Colmar.

21   Long drive to Paris with mid-day stop for a picnic in Reims. Tour Reims' magnificent cathedral with a lesson in Gothic architecture. This is Champagne country and we'll also tour a Champagne cave — free tasting, of course. Evening floodlit orientation tour of Paris with a chance to see all the most famous landmarks.

22   Morning tour of Latin Quarter, Notre Dame, Ile de la Cite, Louvre Museum and historic center of Paris. Afternoon free for more sights or shopping. Evening trip up to Montmartre for a grand view, people-watching, crepes, visit to Sacre Coeur church and free time to enjoy the Bohemian artist's quarter.

Next day. Tour Versailles, Europe's greatest palace.

Your plane will fly you home from Amsterdam ($45 train ride, 5 hours from Paris) on the day of your choice.

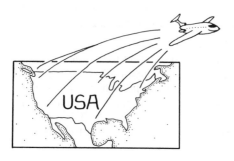

Day 1: Depart USA — Amsterdam

Call before going to the airport to affirm departure time as scheduled. Bring something to do — a book, a journal, some handwork — and make any waits and delays easy on yourself. Remember, no matter how long it takes, flying to Europe is a very easy way to get there.

To minimize jet lag (body clock adjustment, stress):

- Leave well rested. Pretend you are leaving a day earlier than you really are. Plan accordingly and enjoy a peaceful last day.
- During the flight minimize stress by eating lightly, avoiding alcohol, caffeine and sugar. Drink juice.
- Sleep through the in-flight movie — or at least close your eyes and fake it.

Day 2: Arrive in Amsterdam!

When flying to Europe, you always lose a day; if you leave on a Tuesday, when you land it will be Wednesday. Amsterdam's Schiphol Airport, 7 miles out of town, is very efficient and "user friendly." Like nearly every European airport, it has a bank that keeps long hours and offers fair rates. There is also an information desk, plus baggage lockers, on-the-spot car rental agencies, an expensive room-finding service and easy transportation service into the city. Airport taxis are notoriously expensive. Go by bus or train. The airport has a train station of its own. (You can validate your Eurailpass and hit the rails immediately, or pay to get into Amsterdam and start it later.)

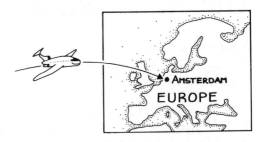

If you are heading for central Amsterdam, a shuttle bus is your best budget bet; for Delft and points south, the train is best — but explore your options at the information desk. Transportation in Holland is great. Buses will take you where trains don't and bicycles will take you where buses don't. Buses and trains both leave from train stations.

The Netherlands

13,000 square miles (Maryland's size).

14 million people (1050 per square mile, compared to 58 per square mile in the USA).

The Netherlands, Europe's most densely populated country, is also one of its wealthiest and best organized. Efficiency is a local custom. The average annual income of $11,700 is higher than America's ($10,740). Forty percent of the work force works with raw materials or in food processing while only 8 percent are farmers. Seventy percent of the land is cultivated, and you'll travel through vast fields of barley, wheat, sugar beets and potatoes. While 40 percent of the Dutch are Catholic and 40 percent are Protestant, church attendance is relatively casual. The Dutch give a larger percent of the GNP away in aid to poor countries than any country on earth.

Holland is the largest of 12 states which make up the Netherlands. To call the country as a whole "Holland" is like calling the USA "Texas." Belgium, the Netherlands, and Luxembourg have united economically to form Benelux. Today you'll find no borders between these "Low Countries" — called that because they're low. Fifty

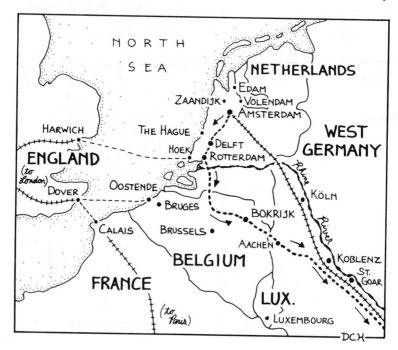

percent of the Netherlands is below sea level, on land that has been reclaimed from the sea. That's why the natives say, "God made the Earth but the Dutch made Holland." Modern technology and plenty of Dutch energy are turning more and more of the sea into fertile farm land.

The state of Holland was a trading superpower and the home of the Northern Renaissance 300 years ago. Today it still shines with the riches, buildings, art and lore of those glorious days.

The Dutch are easy-going, friendly and generally speak very good English. Dutch cities traditionally have been open-minded, loose and liberal, but they are now paying the price of this easy-going style. Amsterdam has become a bit seedy for many travelers' tastes. I enjoy more sedate Dutch evenings by sleeping in a small town nearby and side-tripping into the big city.

The best "Dutch" food is Indonesian (a former colony). Find any "Indish" restaurant and experience a *rijstafel* (rice table) which may have as many as 30 exciting dishes. Local taste treats are cheese, pancakes *(pannekoeken)*, Dutch gin *(jenever)*, beer and "syrup waffles." Yogurt in Holland (and throughout Europe) is delicious and can be drunk right out of its plastic container. Lunch is 12 pm to 2 pm and dinner from 5:30 pm to 9:30 pm.

The country is so small, level and well-covered by trains and buses that transportation is a snap. The excellent train and bus system attracts many visitors. Amsterdam, Rotterdam and The Hague are connected by speedy trains that come and go every 10 or 15 minutes. All you need to enjoy a driving vacation here is a car, gas and a map.

The Netherlands is a bicyclist's delight. The Dutch average four bikes per family, and have put a small bike road beside every big auto route. You can rent bikes at most train stations and can drop them off at most other stations. Shops and banks stay open from 9 am to 5 pm.

Delft: Small-town Headquarters for Holland

Delft, peaceful as a Vermeer painting (he was born there) and lovely as the porcelain it makes, is a safe, pleasant and very comfortable place to overcome jet lag and break into Holland and Europe. Delft is just 60 minutes by train from Amsterdam. Trains depart every half hour, and cost about $8 round trip. While Delft lacks major sights, it is a typically Dutch town with a special soul. You'll enjoy it best just wandering around, watching people, munching, or gazing from the canal bridges into the water and seeing the ripples play games with your face. The town bustles during its Saturday morning market, and also has a great Tuesday market, which attracts many traditional villagers.

Day 2: Arrive Amsterdam

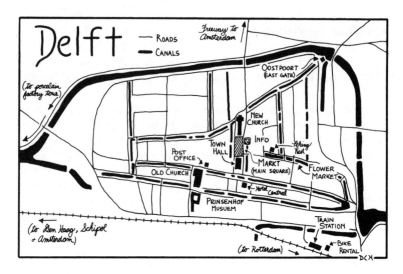

Food and Lodging

Believe me, you don't need to make reservations before you go. Just drop in or call from the airport. Delft has several simple hotels on its market square, the best being Hotel Monopole (Tel. 015-123059. Say hi to Luke. $20 doubles with breakfast; Luke also serves 56 varieties of pancakes. Address: Markt, Delft.)

I sleep at Hotel Central (Wijnhaven 6, 2611 CR, Delft, tel. 015-123442. It runs about $8-10 per person with buffet breakfast, showers, sauna; located between station and square.)

The Peking Chinese-Indonesian restaurant (2 minutes off square, tel 015-141100) serves a grand *rijstafel* Indonesian feast for less than $5. A meal for two could stuff four hungry loggers.

Side Trips

Delft is just a few minutes by train from Rotterdam or The Hague.

Helpful Hints

Remember, if you're returning to Delft at the end of your trip, to reserve a room in your favorite hotel. You can leave any unneeded luggage there free until you return. The free Delft porcelain tour is very interesting as are many sights in The Hague nearby.

While Delft is my choice for an easy first stop in Europe and a good base to see Amsterdam from, it's easy to find a hotel in wild and crazy Amsterdam, if you'd prefer to be where the action is, or in quiet Haarlem, just outside of Amsterdam. Try Hotel Carillon (Grote Market 27, Haarlem, tel. 023-310591. It's $10 per person with breakfast, on main square. Say hi to Franz.)

Day 3: Amsterdam

While Amsterdam has grown a bit "seedy" for many people, it is still worth a full day of sightseeing on even the busiest itinerary. The central train station is your starting point (great tourist information, bike rental, trains to all points) and Damrak is the "main street" axis leading to the Dam Square (people-watching and hang-out center) and to the Royal Palace. The city's major sights are within walking distance of the Dam Square. "Amsterdam in a day" is, if not thorough, very exciting. Plan your time carefully, have a big breakfast and go for it. You'll sleep good that night.

Food and Lodging

Good hotels are expensive. There's no shortage of simple hotels at $10-15 per person (see Arthur Frommer), student crash pads and hostels at $5 per night (see *Let's Go*). Room-finding service at tourist information offices is too expensive. Arrive early and find your own. By afternoon the city can fill up. Best Indonesian restaurants are on Bantammerstraat. Try Ling Nam at #3, just past the "sailor's quarters" (tel. 266579). The Rice Table feast is $5.

Day 3: Amsterdam

Helpful Hints

Monday is a terrible day here. Museums are closed, and shops open only in the afternoon. At tourist information office consider Falk map (best city map), *Amsterdam This Week* (periodical entertainment guide). *Use It* (student and hip guide) lists cheap beds, etc. The trolleys are great, six rides for about $1.50. If you get lost, just ride one back to central train station. Drop by a bar for a *jenever* (Dutch gin) — the closest thing to an atomic bomb in a shot glass.

Sightseeing Highlights

*** **Rijksmuseum** — Start visit with free, short slide show on Dutch art (every 20 minutes all day). Great Rembrandts. Buy the cheap museum map and plan your attack. Bookshop has good posters, prints, slides; there is also a cafeteria and w.c.

*** **Van Gogh Museum** — Next to Rijksmuseum. Outstanding. Beautifully displayed collection of Vincent's work in chronological order. Don't miss it.

Stedelijk Modern Art Museum — Far-out art. Next to Van Gogh. Fun and refreshing.

** **Anne Frank House** — A fascinating look at the hideaway where young Anne hid when the Nazis occupied the Netherlands. Pick up the English pamphlet at the door and don't miss the thought-provoking Neo-Nazi exhibit in the last room.

Royal Palace interior.

Westerkerk — Important old church with Amsterdam's tallest steeple, worth climbing for the view. (Be careful: on a hot day Amsterdam's rooftops sprout nude sun worshippers.) Next to Anne Frank's.

** **Canal Boat Tour** — Boats leave (constantly, everywhere) for the 90-minute, $3 introduction to the city. A good relaxing orientation. Bring a camera.

Begijnhof — A tiny, idyllic courtyard in the city center where the charm of old Amsterdam can still be felt.

Rembrandt's House — Interesting for his fans. Lots of sketches.

Shopping — Waterlooplein (flea market), various flower markets, diamond dealers (free tours). Best walking shopping street is parallel to Damrak.

Heineken Brewery Tours — Crowded, morning only. (9:00 & 11:00).

Red Light District — Europe's most interesting. Near station. Dangerous at night.

Rent a Bike — Around $2 a day, quick and easy at central train station (left end as you leave). Fly through the city with ease (suggested bike tour available at tourist information office). In one day I biked: through red light district, to Our Lord in the Attic (hidden church), to Herrengracht Mansion (at Herrengracht 605, typical old rich household), to Albert Cuypstraat Market (colorful daily street market), to a diamond polishing exhibit and tour (representing many companies), through Vondelpark (Amsterdam's "Central Park," good for people-watching and self-serve cafeteria lunch), to Jordaan district, to Anne Frank's, to Westerkerk (climbed tower), to Royal Palace, and down Damrak back to the station. Whew!

Day 3: Suggested Schedule

9:00 am-10:00 am Anne Frank House, Westerkerk.

10:00 am-11:00 am Palace, Dam Square, walk to Spui on pedestrian-only shopping street. Buy picnic.

11:00 12:30 pm Canal boat tour from Spui.

12:30 pm- 2:00 pm See Begijnhof on way to picnic in Vondelpark.

2:00 pm- 5:00 pm Museums. Divide your time between Rijks, Van Gogh and Modern Art according to your interest.

5:00 pm- 7:00 pm Trolley back to Central Station. Walk through sailors' quarters/red light district to Bantammerstraat for Indonesian dinner.

Side Trips

Many day tours are available from Amsterdam. Buses go to villages from the station. It's important to see small-town Holland. The famous towns (Volendam, Marken Island, Edam, etc.) are very touristy but still fun. Zaandijk has a great open-air folk museum where you can see and learn about cheese and wooden-shoe making. (Hieronymous the shoemaker is a great guy.) Take an inspiring climb to the top of a whirring windmill (get a group of people together and ask for a short tour). You can even buy a small jar of fresh windmill-ground mustard for your next picnic. Zaandijk is a traveler's best one-stop look at traditional Dutch culture and includes the Netherlands' best collection of windmills. (Buses leave from Amsterdam station.)

The energetic can enjoy a rented bicycle tour of the countryside. A free ferry departs from behind the station across the canal. In five minutes Amsterdam will be gone and you'll be rolling through the polderland.

Throughout the Netherlands, the VVV sign means tourist information.

Day 4: From Holland to the Rhine

Today's objective is to get to Germany's Rhineland in the most interesting way. This will be your first European border crossing.

Transportation

By car from Delft, the most rewarding route is through the northeast corner of Belgium (freeway nearly all the way), stopping between Hasselt and Genk to tour the Bokrijk Folk Museum. Driving on, you'll meet the Rhine at Koblenz where it's best to leave the autobahn and take the small riverside road down the Rhine to St. Goar. (Amsterdam-Bokrijk: 3 hours, Bokrijk-St. Goar: 4½ hours.)

By train you can enjoy rural and village Holland for half a day and zip direct to Koblenz in 4 to 4½ hours, and on to St. Goar for dinner. Or you can leave Amsterdam early and stop off in Köln (Germany's greatest gothic cathedral, the impressive Romisch-Germanisches museum and the tourist office are just across the street from the station), Bonn (Germany's peaceful capital city, with a great marketplace and the visit-worthy birthplace of Beethoven), and historic Koblenz where the Rhine and Mosel join forces. There are plenty of trains from Koblenz to St. Goar. (Consider a short stop at Boppard en route.)

Bokrijk

This huge park in the Belgian province of Limburg boasts the biggest and best open-air folk museum in all the Low Countries. Entire villages — not just houses — from the Middle Ages have been reassembled here so visitors can learn about the pillories, thatched roofs, windmills and lifestyles of old. Try to get a guided tour. Otherwise, the English guidebook is your key to understanding what you see.

Bokrijk has much more — including old-fashioned restaurants serving the local equivalent of sassparilla, a zoo, rose garden, nature reserve, youth hostel, and a great opportunity to see Belgian families enjoying life's simple pleasures.

While Bokrijk is in Belgium you won't even know when you've crossed the border. Dutch money is accepted at Bokrijk.

Germany

95,000 square miles (smaller than Oregon).

65 million people (about 650 per square mile, and declining slowly).

Ah, Deutschland. Energetic, efficient, organized and Europe's economic muscleman. Eighty-five percent of its people live in cities and earnings average about $12,400 per year. Ninety-seven percent of the workers get a one-month paid vacation, and during the other eleven months they create a gross national product of about one-third the USA's. Germany is the world's fifth biggest industrial power, ranking fourth in steel output and nuclear power, third in automobile production. It also shines culturally, beating out all but two countries in production of books, Nobel laureates and professors.

While northern Germany is Protestant and the populace assaults life aggressively, southern Germany is Catholic, more relaxed and leisurely. The southern German, or Bavarian, dialect is to High (northern) German what the dialect of Alabama or Georgia is to the northern USA.

Germany's most interesting contemporary tourist route — Rhine, Romantic Road, Bavaria — was yesterday's most important trade

23

Day 4: Holland to the Rhine

route, where Germany's most prosperous and important medieval cities were located. Remember, Germany as a nation is just barely 100 years old. In 1850 there were 35 independent countries in what is now Germany.

Practice your German energetically because nearly half of this tour is in German-speaking countries (Germany, Austria, Switzerland).

Germans eat lunch from 12 pm-3 pm and dinner between 6 pm and 9 pm. Each region has its own gastronomic twist, so order local house specials in restaurants when possible. Fish and venison are good. Great beer and white wines are everywhere. Try the small local brands. "Gummi Bears" are a local gumdrop candy with a cult following (beware of imitations), and *Nutella* is a chocolate nut spread specialty that may change your life.

Banks are generally open 8 am-12:30 pm and 1:30 pm-4 pm, other offices from 8 am to 4 pm. August is a holiday month for workers.

Day 4: (cont'd)

Transportation

The drive to the Rhine will take you past Aachen, Charlemagne's capital city 1200 years ago, and into castle country. At Koblenz you'll cross the Mosel River and follow the smaller road down the west bank of the Rhine in the direction of Boppard. You'll pass castles every few minutes now — first the yellow and rebuilt Stolzenfels, and later across the river the very impressive Marksburg castle. The town of Boppard is worth a short stop and then you'll be in St. Goar.

Food and Lodging

The Rhineland has plenty of budget rooms *(zimmers)* and *Gasthauses* offering fine rooms for $8 to $10 per person, including breakfast. St. Goar, Bacharach and a few other towns have hostels where you'll get a bed for $3. The St. Goar hostel, a big white building directly under the castle, is run very German-style. (Dinners cost about $5 in the small hotels, $3 at the hostel.) Spend the late evening in a *winestube* — soaking up the atmosphere, and some of the local Rhine wine.

I stay one mile north of St. Goar in the friendly, riverside Hotel Landsknecht (tel. 06741-1693). Klaus Nickenig and family charge $10 to $12 per person with breakfast. They offer a special discount to anyone using this book.

The town of Bacharach, near St. Goar, has Germany's best youth hostel — the castle on the hilltop with a royal Rhine view. In Bacharach I'd recommend Hotel Kranenturm for cheap and friendly accommodations and great cooking. Dinner at Altes Haus.

Side Trips

Nearby Aachen is a fun town. Charlemagne's ancient capital, it's one of Germany's most historic and underrated cities.

The Mosel River, which joins the Rhine at Koblenz, is more pleasant and less industrial than the Rhine. Lined with vineyards, tempting villages and two exciting castles (Cochem and Berg Eltz), it's a fine place to spend an extra day if you have one. Cochem is the best home base for the Mosel region.

Day 4: Suggested Schedule

8:00 am-11:00 am	Drive from Delft to Bokrijk.
11:00 am- 2:00 pm	Lunch and tour open-air folk museum.
2:00 pm- 6:00 pm	Drive to St. Goar on the Rhine.
7:00 pm	Dinner at hotel.
9:00 pm-10:00 pm	Evening in St. Goar

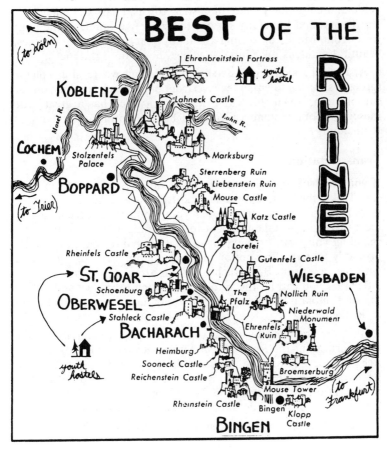

Day 5: The Rhine to Rothenburg

Today can be spent exploring the Rhine's biggest castle, cruising down its most famous stretch and driving on to Rothenberg, Germany's best-preserved medieval town.

The banks open at 8 am in St. Goar. Change enough money to get you through Germany. The Rheinfels Castle is a 15-minute walk up the hill. (You can't miss it; it's the Rhine's biggest and most important castle.) Be there at 9 am when it opens. The castle has several miles of rather spooky tunnels under it. See if there's a guided tour available. The castle shop sells a beautifully illustrated children's book relating the sagas of the Rhine. Buy the foldout tourist's guide map of the Rhine for about $2.

Be back downtown at the Köln-Dusseldorfer boat dock to catch the 10:25 am boat to Bacharach — a one-hour ride upstream ($3 or free with Eurail. You should confirm departure time the night before, from your hotel.) Sit on the top deck with your handy Rhine map-guide and enjoy the parade of castles, towns, boats and vineyards. You'll pass and hopefully survive the seductive Lorelei — the huge rock from which, according to highly placed legendary sources, beautiful maidens once lured medieval boats onto the rocks.

At about 11:30 am you'll de-ship at Bacharach where, after a picnic (grocery shops in town) in the riverfront park, you'll continue on, by car or train, down the Rhine to Mainz (which has a great little museum about Gutenberg and the birth of printing) and on to Rothenburg.

Transportation

If you are driving, taking the boat ride can present a problem. You can (1) skip the boat, (2) take a round-trip tourist excursion boat ride from St. Goar, (3) let one person in your group drive to Bacharach to meet the boat, (4) take the boat to Bacharach and return by train, spending your wait time exploring that old half-timbered town. I'd probably take the first option and spend more time poking around with the car. From Bacharach to Mainz are plenty of good castles. After that you can hit the autobahn, skirting Frankfurt and setting the auto-pilot on Wurzburg. At Wurzburg, take the small road south to Rothenburg.

If you're traveling by train, your Eurailpass gets you onto the Rhine cruise and the *Romantische Strasse* (Romantic Road) bus tour free. The best hour-long cruise of the Rhine is from St. Goar to Bacharach. If you're really enjoying the cruise, stay on to Wiesbaden. If you get off at Bacharach you'll have plenty of trains to take you farther. Ask for schedule information at the boat dock.

The Romantic Road bus tour leaves Wiesbaden at 7 am daily. A

Day 5: The Rhine to Rothenburg

reservation is advisable only on summer weekends. Just telephone 0611-7903240 three days in advance. I think the best part of the trip is south of Rothenburg. You can train to Rothenburg. (This is a bit tricky: Frankfurt to Wurzburg, Wurzburg to Steinach, Steinach to Rothenburg. Get specifics at any German station.) Enjoy an evening in that most romantic of medieval German towns and catch the bus for Munich or Fussen early the next afternoon.

While the Rhine is fine by boat, car and train, it also has a great riverside bicycle path, and it is possible to rent and return bikes at different train stations. This part of the Rhine has no bridges, but plenty of ferries.

Food and Lodging

Rothenburg is crowded with visitors, but finding a room is no problem. From the main square (which has a tourist office with room-finding service), just walk downhill on Schmiedgasse street until it becomes Spitalgasse. This street has plenty of gasthauses, zimmers ($6-10 per person with breakfast) and two fine $3-a-night youth hostels (*Jugendherberge* in German, tel. 09861-4510.) I stay in #28, Hotel zur Goldener Rose, tel. 09861-4638 for about $10 a night. Less expensive yet and very friendly is a room in the home of Herr Moser on Spitalgasse #12.

Day 5: Suggested Schedule

7:30 am	Breakfast.
8:15 am	Banking and browsing in St. Goar.
9:00 am	Tour Rheinfels Castle.
10:25 am	Catch the Rhine steamer, cruise to Bacharach.
11:30 am	Free time for picnic lunch, tour of town.
1:00 pm	Drive to Rothenburg.
5:00 pm	Find hotel and get set up.
Evening	Free in Rothenburg.

Day 6: Rothenburg ob der Tauber

Rothenburg is well worth two nights and a whole uninterrupted day. In the Middle Ages, with a whopping population of 6000, it was Germany's second largest city. Today it's her best-preserved medieval walled town, enjoying tremendous tourist popularity without losing its charm.

Too often Rothenburg brings out the shopper in visitors, before they have had a chance to appreciate the historic city. True, this is a great place to do your German shopping, but first see the town. The tourist information office on the market square has guided tours in English. If none are scheduled, hire a private guide. For about $15, a local historian — who's usually an intriguing character as well — will bring the ramparts alive. A thousand years of history is packed between the cobbles. Sven Schleck (tel. 3856) is my favorite guide. He'll do tours for about $10.

Sightseeing Highlights

First, pick up a map and information at tourist information office on main square (opens at 9 am). Confirm sightseeing plans and ask about tours and evening entertainment.

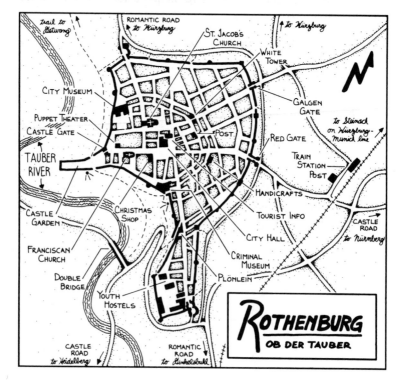

Day 6: Rothenburg ob der Tauber

* **Walk the wall** — 1½ miles around, great views, good orientation. Can be done speedily in one hour. Photographers will go through lots of film. Ideal before breakfast, or at sunset.

** **Climb Town Hall Tower** — Best view of town and surrounding countryside. Opens 9:30 am. Rigorous but interesting climb.

** **Medieval Crime and Punishment Museum** — This is the best of its kind, full of fascinating old legal bits and pieces, instruments of punishment and torture, even a special cage — complete with a metal gag — for nags. Exhibits in English. Open 9:30 am.

*** **St. Jacob's Church** — Here you'll find the best Riemenschneider altarpiece, dated 1466, and located behind the organ. He was the Michelangelo of German woodcarvers. This is the one "must see" art treasure in town.

Be in the main square at 11 am, 12 pm, 9 pm or 10 pm — for the ritual gathering of the tourists to see the reenactment of the *Meistertrunk* story. You'll learn about the town's most popular legend, a fun, if fanciful, story.

Walk in the countryside — The little village of Detwang nearby is actually older than Rothenburg and has another fine Riemenschneider altarpiece.

Rothenburg has some colorful winestubes for your evening fun or you can watch the sun set from the Berggarten Park.

Shopping

Rothenburg is one of Germany's best shopping towns. Make a point to do your shopping here (and mail it home from the handy post office which even sells boxes). Lovely prints, carvings, wine glasses, Christmas tree ornaments and beer steins are very popular. For those who prefer to eat their souvenirs, the *backereis* with their succulent pastries, pies and cakes, are always a distraction. Skip the good looking but bad tasting "Rothenburger Schnee Balls."

Many shops will give you a 10 percent discount on souvenirs if you show them this book and explain to them that you are your own tour guide and would like the normal commission for bringing yourself there. (The shop just west of the tourist office is especially good.)

Day 7: Romantic Road to Dachau to Tyrol

Get an early start to enjoy the quaint hills and rolling villages of this romantic region. What was long ago Germany's major medieval trade route is today's top tourist trip. Stop long enough in Dinklesbuhl for a look around and to buy your picnic. Further south you'll cross the baby Danube River (*Donau* in German) to Dachau. After your picnic, explore the concentration camp and drive through the rest of Bavaria to Reutte in Tyrol, Austria, to make your home base for tomorrow's "castle day" and Bavaria explorations.

Dachau

Dachau was the first Nazi concentration camp (1933). Today it is the most accessible camp to travelers and is a very effective voice from our recent but grisly past, warning and pleading "Never Again" — the memorial's theme. This is a valuable experience, and when approached thoughtfully is well worth the drive — in fact, it may change your life. See it. Feel it. Read and think about it. After this most powerful sightseeing experience, many people are inspired to learn more about contemporary injustices and horrors, and work against tragic reoccurrences.

Upon arrival, pick up the mini-guide and notice when the next documentary film in English will be shown (usually half past each hour). The museum and the movie are worthwhile. Notice the expressionist camp-inspired art near the theater. Outside, be sure to tour the reconstructed barracks and the memorial shrine at the far end. (Near the theater are English books, slides and a good w.c. The camp is open 9 am-5 pm, closed on Mondays.)

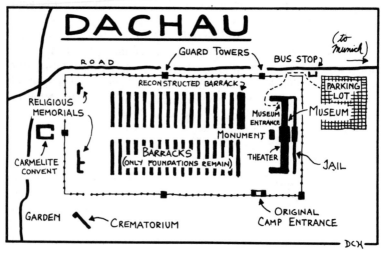

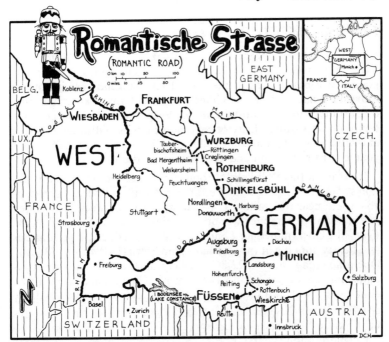

Transportation

By car you'll be following the green "Romantische Strasse" signs, winding scenically through the small towns until you hit the autobahn near Augsburg. Take the autobahn towards Munich ("München") exiting at Dachau. Now follow the signs marked "KZ Gedenkstatte." After Dachau, avoid the Munich traffic by heading for Landsburg and on to Fussen. If the weather's good, drive by Neuschwanstein castle. Just over the border in Austria, you'll find Reutte.

By train pass, catch the Romantic Road bus tour from the Rothenburg train station (or from the *parkplatz*). Two buses come through in the early afternoon. You can catch one bus into Munich (arrives at 6:55 pm) or the other direct to Fussen (arrives at 5:55 pm). Ask about reservations and exact times in Rothenburg at the train station or tourist office. Be early. If you're there when the bus arrives you'll have a better chance of being on it when it leaves two hours later.

Itinerary Options

To save a day you could see Rothenburg during the Romantic Road tour lunch stop and continue south. Munich is a cultural center, capital of Bavaria, and is well worth at least a day if you have the time.

Day 7: Romantic Road

Food and Lodging

In July and August Munich and Bavaria are packed with tourists. Tyrol in Austria is easier and a bit cheaper. Reutte is just one of many good home base towns in the area. I choose it because it's not so crowded in peak season and I like to stay overnight in Austria. Reutte has a good little youth hostel (follow the signs from the town center, a 5-minute walk), and plenty of reasonable hotels and zimmers. I stay at the big, central Hotel zum Goldener Hirsch (tel. 5677-2508) which charges $10 per person and serves great $5 dinners.

In Munich there's a helpful room-finding service in the train station's tourist information office. They can usually find you a reasonable room near the station. If you want a cross between Woodstock and a slumber party for about $2 a night, stay in Munich's "The Tent." In Oberammergau I enjoyed friendly budget accomodations and hearty cooking at the Gasthaus zum Stern (Dorfstrasse 33, 8103 Oberammergau, tel. 08822-867). Oberammergau's youth hostel is unfriendly but very good in all other ways. Countryside guest houses abound in Bavaria and are a great value. Look for signs that say "zimmer frei."

Day 7: Suggested Schedule

8:30 am- 9:30 am Drive from Rothenburg to Dinklesbuhl.

9:30 am-10:00 am Break in Dinklesbuhl town.

10:00 am-12:30 pm Drive on to Dachau, picnic lunch.

1:00 pm- 3:00 pm See Dachau.

3:00 pm- 6:30 pm Drive to Reutte with short stop in Garmisch.

7:30 pm Dinner in guesthouse.

Austria

32,000 square miles (South Carolina's size).

7.6 million people (235 per square mile and holding).

Austria, during the grand old Hapsburg days, was Europe's most powerful empire. Its royalty put together that giant empire of more than 50 million people, not by war but by having lots of children and marrying them into the other royal houses of Europe.

Today Austria is a small landlocked country that does more to cling to its elegant past than any other in Europe. The waltz is still the rage and Austrians are very sociable. More so than anywhere else, it's important to greet people you pass on the streets or meet in shops.

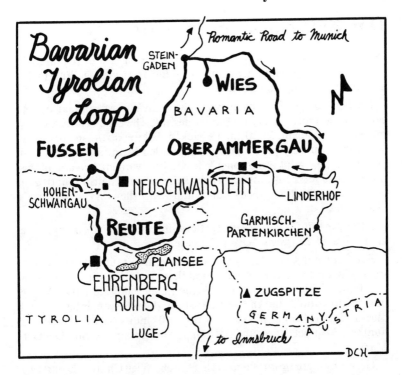

The Austrian's version of Hi is a cheerful *Gruss, Gott!* (May God greet you.)

While they speak German, and German money is readily accepted in Salzburg, Innsbruck and Reutte, the Austrians cherish their distinct cultural and historical traditions. They are not Germans. Austria is mellow and relaxed compared to Deutschland. *Gemütlichkeit* is the special Austrian word for this special Austrian cozy-and-easy approach to life. It's good living — either engulfed in mountain beauty or lavish high culture. The people like to stroll as if every day were Sunday, topping things off with a visit to a coffee or pastry shop. It must be nice to be past your prime — no longer troubled by being powerful, able to kick back and enjoy just being happy in the clean, untroubled mountain air. While the Austrians make less money ($9,000 per year) than their neighbors, they work less (34 hours a week) and live longer (14 percent of the people are senior citizens, the highest percentage in the world).

Austrians eat on about the same schedule as we do. Treats include *Wiener Schnitzel* (breaded veal cutlet), *Knödel* (dumplings), *Apfelstrudel* and fancy desserts. White wines, *Heurigen* (new wine) and coffee are delicious and popular. Shops are open from 8 am-5 pm. Banks keep roughly the same hours, but usually close for lunch.

33

Day 8: Bavaria and Castle Day

Our goal today is to explore two very different castles, Germany's finest rococo-style church, and a typical Bavarian village. We'll make a circular tour starting in Reutte.

It's best to see Neuschwanstein, Germany's most popular castle, early in the morning before the hordes hit. The castle is open every morning at 8:30 am. By 10 am it's packed. Hiking up the steep road to the castle you may pass a crazy old bearded Bavarian. (Hug him if you like, he's a photographer's feast, but women beware of his infamous sauerkraut tongue.) Take the excellent English tour (it gets less excellent as the crowds build) and learn the story of Bavaria's Mad King Ludwig.

After the tour, if you are energetic, climb up to Mary's Bridge for a great view of Europe's "Disney" castle.

Back down in the village you'll find several restaurants. The Jägerhaus is by far the cheapest, with food that tastes that way. Next door is a handy little grocery store. Picnic in the lakeside park. At the intersection you'll find the best gift shop, the bus stop, international dial-direct-to-home phone booths (001-pause-area code-your number. You get 10 seconds of hometown gossip for one Deutsch Mark).

Germany's greatest rococo-style church, Wies Church, is bursting with beauty just 30 minutes down the road. Go north, turn right at Steingaden, and follow the signs. This church is a droplet of heaven, a curly curlicue, the final flowering of the Baroque movement. Read about it as you sit in its splendor, then walk back to the car park the long way, through the meadow.

Oberammergau, the Shirley Temple of Bavarian villages and exploited to the hilt by the tourist trade, has a resilient charm. It's worth a wander. Browse through the wood carvers' shops — small art

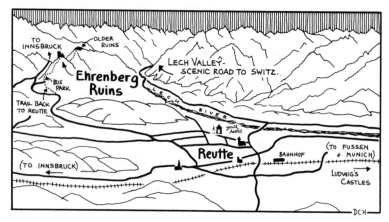

34

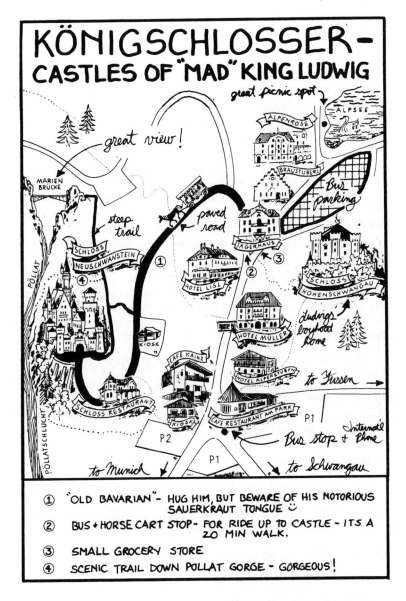

KÖNIGSCHLOSSER –
CASTLES OF "MAD" KING LUDWIG

great picnic spot

ALPSEE

great view!

ALPENROSE

MARIEN BRÜCKE

BRAUSTUBERL

Bus parking

steep trail

paved road

SCHLOSS NEUSCHWANSTEIN

PÖLLAT

JÄGERHAUS

① ③

②

HOTEL LISL

SCHLOSS HOHENSCHWANGAU

④

Ludwig's boyhood home

KIOSK

HOTEL MÜLLER

to Füssen →

CAFE KAINZ

HOTEL ALPENSTUBEN

SCHLOSS RESTAURANT

KIOSK

CAFE RESTAURANT AM PARK

P1

PÖLLATSCHLUCHT

P2

Bus stop & Internat'l Phone

to Munich ↓

P1

to Schwangau

① "OLD BAVARIAN" – HUG HIM, BUT BEWARE OF HIS NOTORIOUS SAUERKRAUT TONGUE ☺

② BUS & HORSE CART STOP – FOR RIDE UP TO CASTLE – ITS A 20 MIN WALK.

③ SMALL GROCERY STORE

④ SCENIC TRAIL DOWN POLLAT GORGE – GORGEOUS!

galleries filled with very expensive whittled works. Visit the church, a cousin of the Wies. Tour the great Passion Play theater. And get out.

Now take the small scenic road past Ludwig's Linderhof Castle. It's the most liveable palace I've seen. Incredible grandeur on a homey scale and worth a look if you have the energy and two or three hours for the tour. Wind past the wind surfer-strewn Plansee, and back into Austria.

Day 8: Bavaria

The road from Reutte to Innsbruck passes the ruined castles of Ehrenberg just outside of town. If the weather's good, drive about four minutes beyond them to the chairlift on the right side of the road. In the summer, this ski slope is used as a luge track. It's one of Europe's great $2 thrills: take the lift up, grab a sled-like go-cart and luge down. The concrete bobsled course banks on the corners and even a novice can go very, very fast. No one emerges from the course without a windblown hairdo and a smile-creased face. (Closed when raining.)

The brooding ruins of Ehrenberg await survivors of the luge. These are a great contrast after this morning's modern castles. Park in the lot at the base of the hill and hike up. It's a 20-minute walk to the small castle, for a great view from your own private ruins. For more castle mystique climb 30 minutes up the neighboring taller hill. Its ruined castle is bigger, more desolate and overgrown, more romantic.

By now it's dinner time, and if you've done all this you'll have a good appetite. Ask in your hotel if there's a Tyroler folk evening tonight. Somewhere in Reutte there should be an evening of yodeling, slap-dancing and Tyrolean frolic — always worth the $3 charge.

Transportation

This day is designed for drivers. Without your own wheels it won't be possible. Local buses serve the area — but not very well. Buses from Füssen station to Neuschwanstein run hourly, $1; Füssen-Wies, twice a day for $3; Oberammergau-Linderhof, fairly regularly. Hitchhiking is possible, but instead I'd take an all-day bus tour from Munich to cover these sights most efficiently.

Itinerary Options

Train travelers may prefer spending this time in Munich and in Salzburg (two hours apart by hourly train). Salzburg holds its own against "castle day" and is better than Innsbruck. Consider a side trip to Salzburg from Munich and the night train from Munich to Venice.

Day 8: Suggested for Circular Car Tour

8:00 am- 8:40 am Drive from Reutte to Neuschwanstein.

9:00 am-10:00 am Tour castle.

10:00 am-12:10 pm Hike, browse, picnic by lake.

12:30 pm- 1:00 pm Visit Wies church.

1:00 pm- 1:30 pm Drive to Oberammergau.

1:30 pm- 3:00 pm Oberammergau (or Linderhof castle).

3:00 pm- 4:00 pm Take bus to luge.

4:00 pm- 5:00 pm Luge experience.

5:00 pm- 7:00 pm Explore two ruined castles.
             8:30 pm Tyrolean folk evening.
        11:30 pm Zzzzzzzzzz.

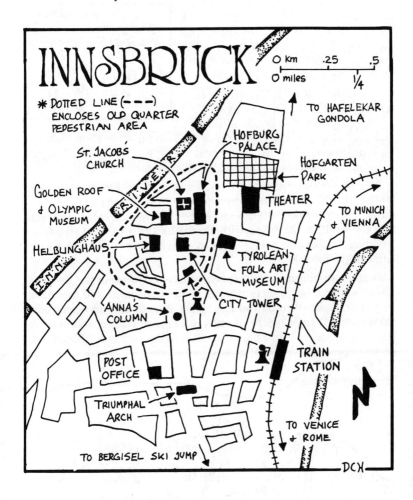

Day 9: Drive over the Alps to Venice

Innsbruck, Western Austria's major city and just a scenic hour's drive from Reutte, is a great place to spend the morning. Park as centrally as possible and give yourself three hours to see the town center and have a picnic lunch.

The Golden Roof is the historic center of town. From this square you'll see a tourist information booth with maps and lists of sights, the newly restored Baroque-style Helblinghaus, the city tower (climb it for a great view), and the new Olympics museum with exciting action videos for winter sports lovers.

Nearby are the palace and church and the very important Tyroler Volkskunst Museum. This museum (open 9 am-12 pm and 2 pm-5 pm daily, closed Sunday afternoons) is the best look anywhere at traditional Tyrolean lifestyles, with fascinating exhibits ranging from wedding dresses and babies' cribs to nativity scenes. Use the helpful English guidebook.

A very popular mountain sports center and home of the 1964 and 1976 Winter Olympics, Innsbruck is surrounded by 150 mountain lifts, 1250 miles of trails and 250 hikers' huts. If it's sunny, consider taking the lift right out of the city to the mountaintops above.

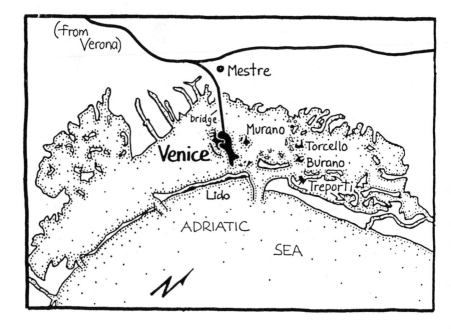

After lunch drive south over the dramatic Brenner Pass. In a surprisingly few minutes you'll cross into Italy and zip out of the Italian mountains, past countless castles, around Romeo and Juliet's hometown of Verona and on to Venice. It's autostrada (superhighway — with tolls) all the way.

Day 9: Suggested Schedule

8:00 am- 9:30 am Drive from Reutte to Innsbruck.

9:30 am-12:30 pm Sightseeing in downtown Innsbruck, lunch.

12:30 pm- 5:30 pm Drive from Innsbruck to Venice.

5:30 pm Take boat #1, the slow boat, down the Grand Canal to San Marco. Find your hotel.

Italy is a whole new world. Now it's time for sunshine, *cappuccino*, *gelati* and *la dolce vita!*

Italy

116,000 square miles (the size of Arizona).

56,000,000 people (477 per square mile).

Ah, Italy! It has Europe's richest, craziest culture — if I had to choose just one. Italy is a blast, if you take it on its terms and accept the package deal. Some people, often with considerable effort, manage to hate it. Italy bubbles with emotion, corruption, inflation, traffic jams, strikes, rallies, holidays, crowded squalor and irate ranters shaking their fists at each other one minute and walking arm in arm the next. Have a talk with yourself before you cross the border. Promise yourself to relax, and soak it in. It's a glorious mud puddle. Be militantly positive.

With so much history and art in Venice, Florence and Rome, you'll need to be a student here to maximize your experience. Italy has two basic halves. The north is relatively industrial, aggressive and time-is-money in its outlook. The Po River basin and the area between Milan, Genoa and Torino is the richest farmland and the industrial heartland. The south is more crowded, poor, relaxed, farm-oriented and traditional. Families here are very strong and usually live in the same house for many generations. The Apennine Mountains give Italy a rugged north-south spine.

Economically, Italy has its problems but things somehow work out. Statistically it looks terrible (high inflation, $7,000 a year average income) but things work wonderfully under the table. Italy is the world's number two wine producer and is number six in cheese and

Day 9: To Venice

wool output. Tourism (your dollars) is a big part of the economy. Only the USA and Spain attract more visitors.

Italy, home of the Vatican, is Catholic but its people put much more visible energy into their love of soccer — especially since their World Cup championship in 1982.

The language is easy. Be melodramatic and move your hand with your tongue. Hear the melody, get into the flow. Fake it, let the farce be with you. Italians are outgoing characters. They want to communicate and try harder than any other Europeans. Play with them.

Italy, a land of extremes, is also the most thief-ridden country you'll visit. Tourists suffer virtually no violent crime — just petty purse-snatching, pick-pocketings and short-changings. Only the sloppy will be stung. Wear your moneybelt! Count your change.

Traditionally, Italy works on the siesta plan: 8 am or 9 am to 1 pm and from 3:30 pm to 7 pm (if the mid-day meal and nap stretch into dinner), six days a week. Many businesses have adopted the government's new recommended 8 am-2 pm work day. In tourist areas, shops are open longer.

While no longer a cheap country, Italy is still a hit with shoppers. Glassware (Venice), gold, silver, leather and prints (Florence) and high fashion (Rome) are good souvenirs.

Many tourists are mind-boggled by the huge price figures: 16,000 lire for dinner! 42,000 for the room! 25,000 for the train ride! That's still real money — it's just spoken of in much smaller units than a dollar. Since there are about 2000 lire in a dollar (at this writing), figure Italian lire prices by covering the last three zeros with your finger and taking half the remaining figure. So that 16,000-lire dinner costs $8 in U.S. money, the room $21, and the train ride about $12.50.

Italians eat a miniscule breakfast, a huge lunch between 12:30 pm and 3:30 pm and a light dinner (quite late). Food in Italy is given great importance and should be thought of as "sight-seeing for your tongue." Focus on regional specialties, wines and pastas. The *gelati* (ice cream) and the coffee is the best anywhere. Have fun in the bars, explore the menus.

La Dolce Far Niente! (The sweetness of doing nothing!) is a big part of Italy. Zero in on the fine points. Don't dwell on the problems. Accept it as a package deal. Savor your cappuccino, dangle your feet over a canal and imagine what it was like a thousand years ago. Look into the famous sculpted eyes of Michelangelo's *David,* and understand Renaissance man's assertion of himself. Ramble through the rubble of Rome and mentally resurrect those ancient stones. Sit silently on a hilltop rooftop. Get chummy with the winds of the past. Write a poem over a glass of local wine in a sun-splashed, wave-dashed Riviera village. Get into it. Be a romantic. Italy is magic.

Day 10: Venice

Soak in this puddle of elegant decay all day long. Venice is Europe's best preserved big city. This car-free urban wonderland of more than one hundred islands, laced together by nearly five hundred bridges, born in a lagoon 1500 years ago as a refuge from barbarians, is overloaded with tourists and slowly sinking (two unrelated facts). In the Middle Ages, after the Venetians smuggled in the bones of St. Mark *(San Marcos)* and created a great trading empire, Venice became Europe's number one economic power. Venice has so much to offer and is worth at least a day on even the speediest tour. This itinerary gives it two nights and a day.

Arriving in Venice

If you've never been there, Venice can be confusing. Actually, even if you have been there, it can be confusing. It's a car-less kaleidoscope of people, bridges and canals. It's like no other city. I wouldn't miss it.

Transportation

By train you'll be dropped at the edge of town where you'll find a helpful tourist information office with maps and a room-finding

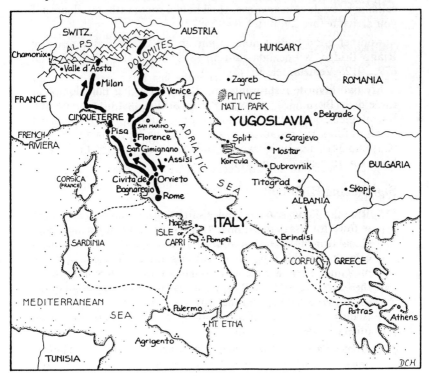

Day 10: Venice

service. In front of the station you'll find the boat dock where the floating "city buses" stop.

By car it's a bit trickier. As the freeway breaks into a swarm of smaller roads, follow the parking lot indicators. There are three or four locations with red or green lights indicating whether or not they have more room. Follow the signs to "Piazza Roma," the most convenient lot, and choose either the huge cheaper open lot or the safer, more expensive high-rise lot right on the square. From there you can visit the tourist information office and catch the boat of your choice deeper into Europe's most enchanting city.

Food and Lodging

Venice is a notoriously difficult place to find a room. You can minimize problems by (1) calling ahead to make a reservation, (2) traveling off season, (3) arriving very early — as you will if you take an overnight train ride from Munich, Vienna or Rome, (4) staying in a mainland town nearby and sidetripping to Venice, (5) using the tourist information office's room-finding service.

Calling ahead is the best idea. My friend Julian Gallo (yep) runs a great budget hotel just two minutes from the main square. His place, Citta di Berna (about $20 for a double), fills up nearly every day, so call him a few days in advance. He'll hold a room without a deposit if you arrive before 2 pm (tel. 041-25872).

Another good budget hotel, right on the Grand Canal near the Rialto Bridge, is Locanda Sturion (S. Polo, Rialto, Calle Sturion 679, 30125 Venizia. tel. 36243).

My two favorite restaurants are: Rosticceria San Bartolomeo at Calle della Bissa 5424, near the Rialto Bridge, just off Campo San Bartolomeo (busy, cheap, self-serve on ground floor, great budget meals in full-serve restaurant upstairs) and the Trattoria de Remigio (Castello 3416, tel. 30089; wonderfully local and in a great neighborhood for after-meal wandering).

Sightseeing Highlights

*** **Ride the *Vaporettos*** — Venice's floating city buses to anywhere in town for less than $1. Boat #1 is the slow boat down the Grand Canal (for the best do-it-yourself introductory tour). Number 5 offers a circular tour of the city (get off at Murano for glass-blowing). There are plenty of boats leaving from San Marco to the beach *(Lido)* as well as speedboat tours of Burano (a quiet, picturesque fishing and lace town), to Murano (glass-blowing island) and to Torcello (oldest churches and mosaics on an otherwise desolate island).

*** **Doge's Palace** — The former ruling palace has the second largest wooden room in Europe, virtually wallpapered by Tintoretto,

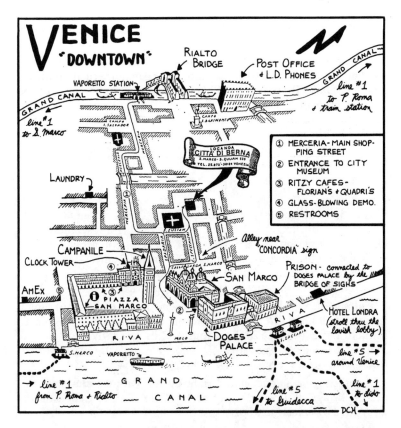

Titian and other great painters. Nearby is the Bridge of Sighs and the prison (open 9 am-4:30 pm). No tours; buy guidebook in street.

** St. Mark's Basilica — For 1100 years it has housed the Saint's bones. Study the floor, treasures, and views from the balcony. Modest dress (no shorts) usually required.

** Campanile — Ride the elevator ($1) up 300 feet for the best possible view of Venice. Notice photos on wall inside showing how tower fell 80 years ago. Be on top when the bells ring for a most ear-shattering experience (ask about hours). Open all day.

Bell Tower — See the bronze men in action. Open from 9 am-12 pm and 3 pm-6 pm. Notice the world's first "digital" clock on the tower facing St. Mark's Square.

*** Accademia — Venice's greatest art museum is packed with the painted highlights of the Venetian Renaissance. Just over the wooden Accademia Bridge, open 9 am-2 pm.

* Basilica dei Frari — A great church housing Donatello's wood-carving of David and much more.

Day 10: Venice

* **Scuola di San Rocco** — Next to the Frari church, another lavish building bursting with art, including some 50 Tintorettos.

  Peggy Guggenheim Collection — A popular collection of far-out art that so many try so hard to understand. Includes works by Dali, Picasso and Pollock. Open 2 pm-6 pm, closed Tuesdays.

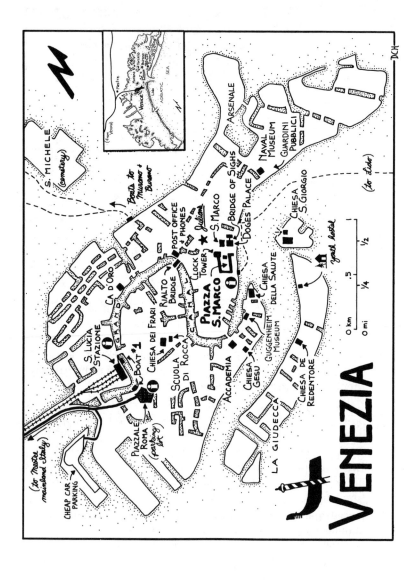

Day 10: Venice

Helpful Hints

About wandering in Venice: Walk and walk, get as lost as possible. Notice how Venice is shaped like a fish. Explore the tail. Keep reminding yourself, "I'm on an island and I can't get off." When it comes time to find your way, look for arrows on walls at street corners to landmarks (San Marco, Rialto, etc.) or simply ask a local, *Dove* (DOH' vay) *San Marco?* (Where is St. Mark's?).

Try a siesta in the Giardini Pubblici (public gardens, in the tail area), on the Isle of Burano, or in your hotel.

The best shopping area is around the Rialto Bridge and along the Merceria, the road connecting St. Mark's and the Rialto.

Day 10: Suggested Schedule

8:00 am Breakfast.

8:30 am Drop laundry off at laundromat, walk through town.

9:00 am Basilica dei Frari and Scuola di San Rocco — for art lovers.

11:00 am Accademia Gallery.

12:30 pm Lunch.

2:00 pm St. Mark's area — tour Doge's Palace, Basilica, ride to top of Campanile.

5:30 pm Collapse in hotel after picking up laundry.

8:00 pm Dinner or commence pub crawl.

Evening: The stand-up-progressive-Venetian-pub-crawl-dinner

Venice's residential back streets hide plenty of characteristic bars with plenty of interesting toothpick munchie food. This is a great way to mingle and have fun with the Venetians. The best pubs are in the castello district near the Arsenal. The Italian word for hors d'oeuvres is *ciquita* (pronounced Chick EE' ta, like the banana). They wait under glass in every bar. Try fried mozzarella cheese, blue cheese, calamari, artichoke hearts and the house wines. When you're good and ready, ask for a glass of *grappa,* the beef jerky of Italian wine. Bars don't stay open very late so start your evening by 8 pm. Ask your hotel manager for advice — or to join you.

Nighttime is the right time in Venice. My favorite hotel, Citta di Berna, is a two-minute walk from San Marco's. Soft summer nights, live music, floodlit history, a ceiling of stars, make St. Mark's magic at midnight. Be there, be romantic, soak in it.

Day 11: Florence

Today there are two goals: (1) travel from Venice to Rome, and (2) see Florence. Okay, of course you can't really see Florence in a day, but you can do pretty well. It's three hours by train or car from Venice to Florence and three more hours to Rome. If you leave early and arrive late you'll have seven or eight hours in Florence. So here's the plan: Leave Venice at the crack of dawn (don't wait for your hotel's skimpy breakfast). Even the pigeons will be sleepy as you march through the empty dawn streets. By 10:30 am you'll be in Europe's art capital.

Florence requires organization — especially for a blitz tour. Most important, remember that some attractions close early, while others are open all day. Everything is within walking distance of the station and the town center. Our suggested walk starts at the Accademia (home of Michelangelo's masterpiece, *David*), and cuts through the heart of the city to the Ponte Vecchio (old bridge) on the Arno River. See everyone's essential sight, *David,* right off. In Italy a masterpiece in the hand is worth two down the street; you never know when they'll unexpectedly lock up the Accademia. Then walk down the street to the Cathedral, or Duomo. Check out the famous doors and the interior of the Baptistry and cross the street to the tourist office where you can doublecheck the hours of the rest of the city's sights. Farther down that street visit the Or San Michele church and grab a quick lunch nearby. Around the corner is the central square (Piazza della Signoria), the city palace (Palazzo Vecchio) and the great Uffizi Gallery — all very important.

After you walk past the statues of the great men of the Renaissance in the Uffizi courtyard, you'll get to the Arno River and the Ponte Vecchio. Your introductory walk will be over, but your Florence experience will have just begun. After the overview, you'll still have half a day to see a lifetime of art and history — or just to shop, people-watch and enjoy Europe's greatest ice cream. Here are a few ideas:

Sightseeing Highlights

*** **The Accademia** — Houses Michelangelo's *David* and his powerful *Prisoners.* Eavesdrop as tour guides explain these masterpieces. There's also a lovely Botticelli painting. (Open Tues.-Sat. 9 am-2 pm, Sun. 9 am-1 pm, closed Monday.) Be careful: most Italian museums allow the last visitors in 30 minutes before closing. There's a great book and poster shop across the street.

Day 11: Florence

* **San Marco** — Next to the Accademia, this museum houses the greatest collection anywhere of dreamy medieval frescos, painted by Fra Angelico. You'll see why he thought of his painting as a form of prayer. Also see Savonarola's monastic cell.

** **The Duomo** — The cathedral of Florence is a mediocre Gothic building capped by a magnificent Renaissance dome — the first Renaissance dome, by Brunelleschi, and the model for domes to follow. (When working on St. Peter's in Rome, Michelangelo said, "I can build a dome bigger but not more beautiful than the dome of Florence.") You can climb to the top but I'd recommend climbing Giotto's Tower next to it — faster, not so crowded and better view (including dome). Tower is open 8:30 am-12:30 pm, 2:30 pm-5:30 pm.

** **Museo del Duomo** — The Cathedral Museum, just behind the church at #9, has many Donatello statues and a Michelangelo *Pieta*. Great if you like sculpture. (Mon.-Sat. 9:30 am-1 pm, 2:30 pm-5:30 pm, Sun. 10 am-1 pm.

** **The Baptistry** — Michelangelo said its gates were fit for paradise. Check out the famous carved bronze doors by Ghiberti — a breakthrough in perspective and 3-D sculpture on a 2-D surface. Go inside for the medieval mosaic ceiling. Compare that to the "new improved" art of the Renaissance.

Or San Michele — Mirroring Florentine values, it's a combination church-grainery. Notice the spouts for grain to pour through the pillars inside. Also study the sculpture on its outside walls. You can see man literally stepping out in the work of the great Renaissance sculptor, Donatello.

* **Palazzo Vecchio** — The fortified palace of the Medici family. If you've read your history, this is exciting — otherwise skip it. Open 9 am-7 pm.

*** **Uffizi Gallery** — The greatest collection of Italian painting anywhere. A must with plenty of works by Lippi, Bronzino, Caravaggio, Rubens, Goya, Titian, Michelangelo and a roomful of Botticellis — a sight from which you may never recover. There are no tours, so buy a book on the street before entering. (Open all day, 9 am-7 pm; Sun. 9 am-1 pm; closed Monday). Enjoy the Uffizi square full of artists, souvenir stalls and all the surrounding statues of the earth-shaking Florentines of 500 years ago.

** **Bargello** — The city's greatest sculpture museum is just behind the palace. Donatello's *David,* Michelangelo works, much more. Very underrated. Open 9 am-2 pm, closed Monday.

* **Medici Chapel** — Incredibly lavish High Renaissance architecture and sculpture by Michelangelo. Open all day, surrounded by lively market scene.

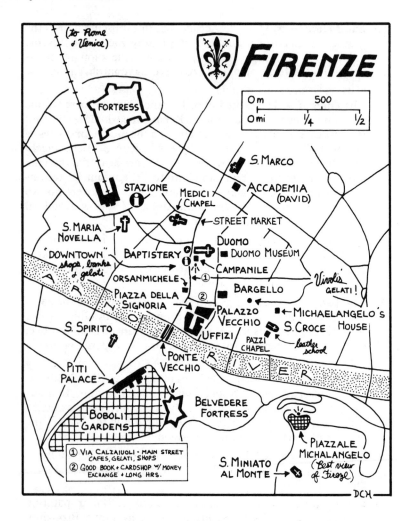

*   **Michelangelo's Home** — Fans will enjoy his house on Ghibellina, #70.

*   **The Pitti Palace** — Across the river, it has a giant art collection with works of the masters, plus more modern Italian art (lovely) and a huge garden.

There's much, much more. Buy a guidebook. Doublecheck your plans with the tourist office. Remember, many museums call it a day at 2 pm and let no one in after 30 minutes before closing. Most are closed Monday, and at 1 pm on Sunday.

Best views of Florence are from Piazza Michelangelo (30-minute uphill walk, across the river), from the top of the Duomo or Giotto's Tower, and in the poster and card shops.

Shopping

Florence is a great shopping town. Busy street scenes and markets abound (especially San Lorenzo, the Mercato Nuovo, on the bridge, and near Santa Croce). Leather, gold, silver, art prints and tacky "mini-Davids" are most popular. Of course, *gelati* is a great Florentine art form. Italy's best ice cream is in Florence (especially at Vivoli's — see map). That's one souvenir that won't clutter your luggage.

Food and Lodging

Florence is one of Europe's most crowded, difficult and overpriced cities when it comes to finding a meal and a bed. The easiest plan is *not* to sleep here. If you do need a bed, call ahead or arrive early and take advantage of the tourist office near the station.

While there are some special budget restaurants listed in most guidebooks, in Florence I keep it fast and simple, lunching in one of countless self-serve joints or picnicking (juice, yogurt, cheese, roll: $2).

Day 11: Suggested Schedule

6:30 am	Leave Venice hotel without breakfast, catch canal boat.
7:15 am	Catch train or drive to Florence (breakfast en route).
11:00 am- 5:00 pm	Sightsee Florence.
5:00 pm- 8:30 pm	Take train or drive south to Rome.
8:30 pm	Check into hotel, collapse. (Don't arrive in Rome late without a reservation.)

Transportation

By car, traveling from Venezia (Venice) to Roma (Rome) via Firenze (Florence) is quite easy. It's autostrada (with reasonable tolls) all the way. From Venice, follow the signs to Bologna and then head for Firenze. Parking in Florence is horrendous at best. Ideally, you can park in the Piazza della S.S. Annunziata lot just behind the Accademia. Otherwise, park where you can and catch a cab to the Accademia. To leave, follow the green signs to Roma.

At the edge of Rome, there's a freeway tourist office. If open, use their great room-finding service, confirm sightseeing plans and pick up a map while you're at it. Take the Via Saleria exit and work your way doggedly into the Roman thick of things. Avoid driving in Rome during rush hour. (You may find every hour is rush hour but some are even worse than others.) Parking in Rome is dangerous. Choose a well-lit busy street or a safe neighborhood. My favorite hotel is next to the Italian "Pentagon" — guarded by machine-gunners. In Rome,

Day 11: Florence

when all else fails, hire a cab and follow him to your hotel.

By train things are much easier. The Venice-Florence-Rome trains are fast and frequent, zipping you straight into the centrally located station. Use train time to eat, study and plan.

Optional Itinerary

Taking in Venice, Florence, Rome — bing, bing, bing — is asking for sensory overload. Especially by train. It might be preferable to do Venice, take the night train to Rome, see the hill towns and go on to Florence. Or, you could make Florence a home base for some small-town exploring before you hit Rome, or more peacefully, make a small town (like Arezzo) your home base, and sidetrip into Florence as well as into the surrounding countryside before plunging into Rome. By seeing the hilltowns on your way south, you could night-train from Rome directly to the Italian Riviera.

Food and Lodging

Rome is difficult only because of its overwhelming size. There are plenty of *pensioni* for budget ($10 per person) beds. In Rome I often get a nicer place — spending more money — for its peaceful oasis/refuge value. The convents of the city are your most interesting budget bet. (They operate tax-free, so are cheaper.) These are obviously peaceful, safe and clean, but sometimes stern and usually "no speak English." Try the Suore di Sant Anna (Piazza Madonna dei Monti #3, 00184 Roma, tel. 06-485778). Three blocks from the Forum near via Serpentine is a place for Ukrainian pilgrims — not a privileged class in the USSR — and therefore they rarely visit, and these lodgings are usually empty. The residents speak Italian, Portuguese and, of course, Ukrainian — good luck. If you land a spot, it's great atmosphere, great meals, great location and great price.

Near the Vatican Museum on #42 via Andrea Doria is the *Suore* (convent) Oblate Dell Assunzione (tel. 3599540, $6 per night, no meals). Spanish, French and Italian spoken in a fun neighborhood across from a colorful market. My choice for more normal accommodations is Pension Nardizzi (via Firenze #38, 00184 Roma, tel. 06-460368.) It's in a safe, handy and central location, 5-minute walk from central station and Piazza Barberini near via XX Septembre. It's expensive ($17 bed and breakfast) but worth the splurge if you've got the urge. Sr. Nardizzi speaks English.

Otherwise the area around the station seethes with accommodations of all styles. Do arrive early or call ahead if possible. The central station *(Termini)* is a jack of all trades with a bank that's open late, tourist information, room-finding service, a day hotel, subway station and major city bus station. Pick up the periodical entertainment guide, *Qui Roma* (Here's Rome).

Days 12-13: Rome

Rome is magnificent. Your ears will ring, your nose will turn your Kleenex black, you'll be run down or pick-pocketed if you're sloppy enough, and you'll be frustrated by chaos that only an Italian can understand. But you must see Rome. If your hotel provides a comfy refuge; if you pace yourself, accepting and even partaking in the siesta plan; if you're well-organized for sightseeing; and if you protect you and your goodies with extra caution and discretion, you'll do fine. You may see the sights and leave satisfied — you may even fall in love with the Eternal City.

Rome wasn't built in a day — nor can it be seen in a day — so we'd suggest taking two. Focusing selectively on the highlights of Ancient Rome, Baroque Rome and the Vatican, two well-organized days can be very productive.

(A general mid-trip note: I assume I've already lost the readers who refuse to accept blitz travel as a realistic option for the over-worked American who can get two weeks off and "call in well" for a third if he's lucky, and who desperately wants to see the all-stars of European culture. So we'll unashamedly accept our time limitations and do our darndest — resting when we get home.)

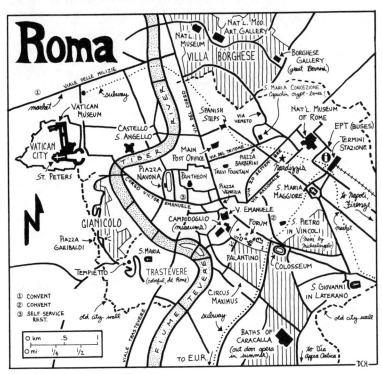

Days 12 and 13: Suggested Schedule

Day 1

7:45 am	Breakfast
8:30 am	St. Peter in Chains Church to see Michelangelo's *Moses* (admittedly out of historical sequence but it opens at 8 am and is a short walk from the Colosseum which opens at 9 am).
9:00 am- 9:45 am	Colosseum.
10:00 am-11:30 am	Roman Forum.
11:30 am- 1:00 pm	Mammartine Prison, Capitoline Hill (Campidoglio) square by Michelangelo and museums (history and sculpture), Piazza Venezia, Victor Emmanuel Monument.
1:00 pm- 3:00 pm	Return to hotel, self-serve restaurant (ask receptionist for recommendation) and siesta.
3:30 pm- 6:00 pm	St. Peter's Cathedral — church, crypt, hike to top of dome, treasury, square, post office.
6:30 pm- 9:00 pm	Explore Trastevere, dinner in small neighborhood restaurant (open for dinner at 8 pm).
9:00 pm-11:00 pm	Walk home — Santa Maria church (Trastavere), Tiber Island, Piazza Navona (*tartufo* ice cream at Tre Scalinis), Pantheon, Trevi Fountain (toss in three coins if you must), Spanish Steps (very overrated, best at night), and home. Catch a taxi early if you run out of steam.

Day 2

8:00 am	Breakfast.
9:00 am- 9:45 am	Pantheon.
10:00 am- 1:00 pm	Allow free time for additional sightseeing or shopping and lunch.
1:30 pm- 4:00 pm	Vatican museum.
4:00 pm	Leave Rome for hill towns, two hours north.

Transportation

Day 1: Walk from St. Peter's in chains to Piazza Venezia, take cab or bus to hotel. Then go by cab or bus back to the Vatican and to Trastevere (Santa Maria). Walk from Santa Maria to hotel or finish early with taxi.

Day 2: Use taxis or buses. Take subway from Vatican (Ottaviano stop) to train station (Terminal).

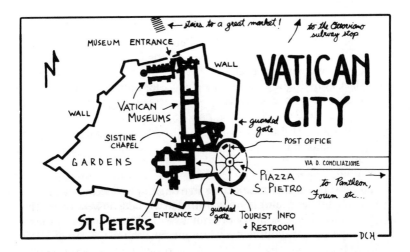

Helpful Hints

Shops and offices are open 9 am-1 pm, 4 pm-8 pm; churches from 8 am-1 pm; museums, 9 am-2 pm, closed at 1 pm on Sundays and closed on Mondays. Outdoor sights like the Colosseum, Forum and Ostia Antica, are open 9 am-7 pm, often closed one day a week. The Capitoline Hill museums are Rome's only nocturnal museums, open Tuesdays and Thursdays, 5 pm-8 pm and Saturdays 8:30 pm-11 pm. There are no absolutes in Italy and these hours may vary inexplicably. In the holiday month of August, many shops and restaurants close up.

Sightseeing Highlights

San Pietro in Vincoli (St. Peter in Chains) Church — On exhibit are the original chains and Michelangelo's *Moses*. This is one of the few sights that opens before 9 am. Here and throughout Italy, use the recorded information boxes — just dial English and put in 200 lire. If you haven't already, buy the little $2 Rome book with map.

*** **Colosseum** — THE great example of Roman engineering, 2000 years old. Putting two theaters together, the Romans created an amphitheater capable of seating 50,000 people. Read up on it. Climb to the top. Subway stops here. Watch out for gypsy thief gangs — usually very young timid-looking girls.

*** **Foro Romano (Roman Forum)** — The civic center of the city and its birthplace. The common ground of the seven hills. Climb the Palatino Hill (where the emperor's palaces were) for a great view, and mentally piece together the rubble of the Forum with the help of the artist's reconstruction in your $2 guidebook. For the studious, special Forum guidebooks are available.

Mamertine Prison — The 2500-year-old converted cistern which once imprisoned Saints Peter and Paul is worth a look. On the walls are lists of prisoners (Christian and non-Christian) and how they were executed. At the top of the stairs leading to the Campidoglio you'll find a cool water fountain. Use it. Block the spout with your fingers — it spurts up for drinking. You'll look quite Roman.

* **Capitoline Hill (Campigoglio)** — The famous square designed by Michelangelo is three-sided (OK, it's not really a square), with two fine museums and the mayoral palace facing each other. The museum closest to the river is most important. Outside the entrance, notice the marriage announcements. You'll probably see a few blissfully attired newlyweds as well. Inside the courtyard have some photo fun with chunks of a giant statue of Emperor Constantine. (A w.c. is hidden around the corner.) The museum is worthwhile, with lavish rooms housing several great statues including the original (500 B.C.) Etruscan she-wolf. Across the square is a museum full of ancient statues — great if you like protrait busts of forgotten emperors.

As you walk down the grand stairway toward Piazza Venezia, notice the cage on your right housing the city's mascot, the she-wolf. At the bottom of the stairs, look up the long stairway to your right for a good example of the earliest style of Christian church — and be thankful you don't need to climb those steps. Farther on, look into the ditch (on the right) and see how everywhere modern Rome is built upon the countless bricks and forgotten mosaics of ancient Rome. Down the street on your left you'll see a modern building actually built around surviving ancient pillars and arches.

Piazza Venezia — This square is the focal point of modern Rome. The via del Corso, starting here, is the city's axis (surrounded by the classiest shopping district). From the balcony above the square, Mussolini aroused the nationalistic fervor of Italy, and the masses filled the square screaming, "Right on! Il Duce!"

Victor Emmanuel Monument — Loved only by the ignorant and his relatives, most Romans call this huge chunk of touristic tofu in a cultural candy shop, "the wedding cake" or "the typewriter." It wouldn't be so bad if it weren't sitting on a priceless piece of Ancient Rome.

*** **Pantheon** — The greatest look at the splendor of Rome, this best-preserved interior of antiquity is a must (open 9 am-1 pm, 2 pm-6 pm, closed Monday). Sit inside and study it. Its dome, 140 feet high and wide, was Europe's largest until Brunelleschi's dome was built in Florence 1200 years later. In a little square to the left, past the Bernini elephant and Egyptian obelisk statue, is a small church with a little-known Michelangelo statue.

** **Piazza Navona** — Rome's most interesting night scene if you like street music, artists, fire eaters, local Casanovas, great ice cream *(tartufo),* outdoor cafes, hippies, and a fine Bernini fountain (he's the father of Baroque art), in an oblong square molded around a long-gone ancient chariot race track. Don't joke around with the bulletproof-vested machine gunner you'll pass as you walk toward the Pantheon.

* **Villa Borghese** — Rome's "Central Park" is great for people-watching (plenty of modern Romeos and Juliets). You can have a row in the lake and visit museums containing fantastic Baroque paintings, an Etruscan collection and modern art.

* **National Museum of Rome** — Directly in front of the station, it houses the greatest ancient Roman sculpture.

* **Trastevere** — The best look at old modern Rome. Colorful street scenes: pasta rollers, street-wise cats, crinkly old political posters encrusting graffiti-laden walls. There are motionless men in sleeveless T-shirts framed by open windows, cobbles with centuries of life ground into their cleavages, kids kicking soccer balls into the cars that litter their alley-fields. The action all marches to the chime of the church bells. Go there and wander. Wonder. Be a poet.

** **Ostia Antica** — Rome's ancient seaport (100,000 people in the time of Caesar, later a ghost town, now excavated) is the next best thing to Pompeii, and, I think, Europe's most underrated sight. Start at the 2000-year-old theater, buy a map, explore the town, finishing with its fine little museum. Get there by subway from downtown. Just beyond is the beach *(Lido)* — interesting, but crowded and filthy.

The Vatican City — The world's smallest independent country is contained within Rome. Politically powerful, the Vatican is the religious capital of 800 million Roman Catholics. It deserves maximum respect regardless of your religious beliefs.

*** **St. Peter's Basilica** — There is no doubt: this is the biggest, richest and most impressive cathedral on earth. To call it vast is an understatement; marks on the floor show where the next largest churches would fit if they were put inside. The ornamental cherubs would dwarf a large man. Birds roost inside, and thousands of people wander about, heads craned heavenward, hardly noticing each other. Don't miss Michelangeleo's *Pieta* to the right of the entrance. Bernini's altar work and huge bronze canopy are brilliant (open 7 am-6 pm daily). The Treasury and the crypt are also important (open 9 am-12:30 pm, 3 pm-4:30 pm). English guided tours (free) are offered daily. The tour I took was really the best I've ever had. A guidebook is essential. The dome, Michelangelo's last work, is (of course) the biggest anywhere. Taller than a football field is long, it is well worth the climb (537 steps) for a great view of Rome, of the Vatican

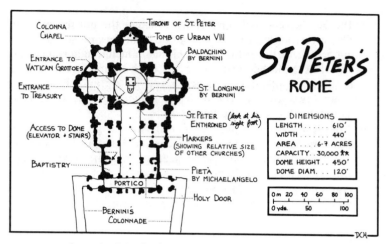

grounds and of the inside of the Cathedral (open 8 am-4:45 pm daily). Remember to dress modestly — long pants or dress, shoulders covered.

*** **The Vatican Museum** — Too often treated as an obstacle course separating the tourist from the Sistine Chapel, this is one of Europe's top three or four houses of art. It can be exhausting, so plan your visit carefully, focusing on a few themes, and allow several hours. (I'd recommend Etruscan, Egyptian, Pio-Clementine collection, modern Catholic art, Raphael and the Sistine.) The museum clearly marks out four color-coded visits of different lengths. Remember it's one way only, so when you get to the Sistine Chapel you can't backtrack. Rent the headphones ($1) before the Raphael rooms to get a recorded tour of these and Michelangelo's Sistine masterpiece. These rooms are the pictorial culmination of the Renaissance (open 9 am-4 pm, closed Sundays).

The museum book and card shop is great, offering, for example, a priceless black-and-white photo book of the *Pieta,* which I stock up on for gifts. The museum and the Piazza San Pietro have a Vatican post office with comfortable writing rooms. The Vatican post is the only reliable mail service in Italy (it must go via the Holy Ghost) and the stamps are a collectible bonus.

Street Market — In front of the Vatican Museum is my favorite Roman market: people, fruits and vegetables.

Capuchin Crypt — Below Santa Maria della Concezione on Via Veneto near Piazza Barberini. If you want bones, this is it. There are thousands of skeletons all artistically arranged for the delight or disgust of the always wide-eyed visitor. Do read the monastic message so you'll understand this as more than just an exercise in bony gore. Pick up a few of Rome's most interesting postcards. (open 9 am-12 pm, 3 pm-6:30 pm).

E.U.R. — Mussolini's planned suburb of the future (50 years ago) is just a ten-minute subway ride from the Colosseum. Very impressive with a great history museum including a large scale model of ancient Rome.

Overrated Sights — Spanish Steps and Trevi Fountain (but very central, free and easy to see). The Catacombs — no bones, way out of the city, commercialized.

Helpful Hints

Place to meet a rich and sexy single Italian (or just look): the street-side cafes of Via Veneto.

For Tired Tourists: taxis are not expensive if the meter is turned on. Subways require coins and nobody within 100 yards will give you change. Save time and legwork whenever possible by telephoning. When the feet are about to give out, sing determinedly, "Roman, Roman, Roman, keep those doggies movin'. . ."

Hotels can recommend the best nearby cafeteria or restaurant. A handy self-serve is Il Delfino, corner of Via Argentina and Via Vittorio Emmanuel near the Pantheon. Also near the Pantheon (two blocks in front down Via Maddalena, around the corner to the left) is Hostaria la Nuova Capannina, on Piazza della Coppelle #8, close to Pantheon, with good, budget sit-down meals. If your convent serves food, eat it; it's heavenly. Avoid restaurants on any famous square. In Trastevere I enjoyed Il Comparone on Piazza in Piscinula #47, tel. 5816249. Near the Piazza Navona try the restaurants on Campo Fiori.

The Great Escape

OK, the 22-day plan is to head for the hilltowns to end Day Number 13. Drive one hour north to Orvieto then leave the freeway and under the evening sun, wind through fields and farms to Bagnoregio, where locals will direct you to Angelino Catarcia's Al Boschetto, the only hotel in town ($15-20 per double, bed and breakfast). Angelino doesn't speak English; he doesn't need to. Have an English-speaking Italian call him for you from Rome, (tel. 0761-9369. Address: Strada Monterado, Bagnoregio, Viterbo, Italy). His family is wonderful and if you so desire, he'll get the boys together and take you deep into the gooey, fragrant bowels of "The Cantina." Music and vino kills the language barrier in Angelino's wine cellar. Angelino will teach you his theme song, "Trinka, Trinka, Trinka." The lyrics are easy (see previous sentence). Warning: descend at your own risk. If you are lucky enough to eat dinner at Angelino's ("bunny" is the house specialty), ask to try the *dolce* (sweet) dessert wine.

When you leave the tourist crush, life as a traveler in Italy becomes very easy. You should have no trouble finding rooms in the small towns of Italy. You won't even need a list, or recommendations.

Day 14: Italian Hilltowns

Today is devoted to rural and small-town Italy — more specifically, to the province of Umbria which, along with Tuscany is noted for its enchanting time-passed towns and villages. Driving from Bagnoregio towards Orvieto, we'll stop just past Purano to tour an Etruscan tomb. Follow the yellow road signs, reading Tomba Etrusca, to Giovanni's farm (a sight in itself). Find the farmer and he'll take you out

back and down into the lantern-lit 1500-year-old tomb. His Italian explanation is fun. Tip him a dollar or two and drive on to Orvieto.

Orvieto, Umbria's grand hilltown, is no secret but well worthwhile. Study its colorful Italian Gothic cathedral with exciting Signorelli frescos. Across the street are a fine Etruscan museum, a helpful tourist office and unusually clean public toilets. Orvieto is famous for its ceramics and its wine.

Drive back to the edge of Bagnoregio, where you'll park your car and walk the steep donkey path to the traffic-free, 2500-year-old, vast, canyon-swamped, pinnacle-town of Civita di Bagnaregio. This town is magic, handle it carefully! Al Forno (green door on main square) is the only restaurant in town, and it's great for lunch. Ask for Anna there for a tour of the little church (tip her and buy your post cards from her). A cute little museum (ask for moo-ZAY'-oh) is just around the corner. Around the other corner is a cool and friendly

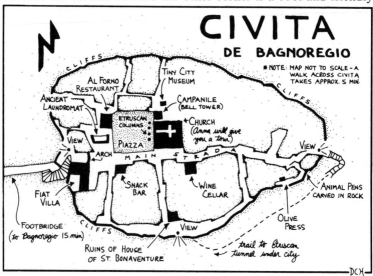

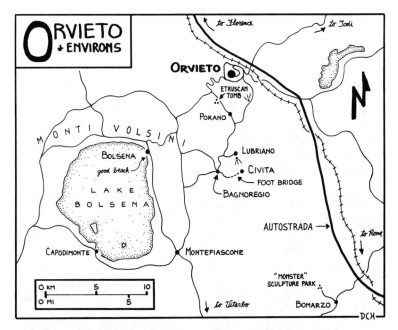

wine cellar, serving local wine on a dirt floor with stump chairs for 20 cents a glass. Civita offers lots more; it's an Easter egg hunt and you're the kid.

Day 14: Suggested Schedule

8:30 am	Breakfast
9:00 am-10:00 am	Drive to Etruscan tomb and tour it.
10:30 am-12:30 pm	Orvieto.
1:00 pm- 4:00 pm	Free time in Civita di Bagnoregio.
Evening	Further exploration by car, or rest in hotel. Be sure you aren't missing any nearby fiestas.

Optional Itinerary

If you are traveling by train, touring the hilltowns will be much more difficult. Italy's small-town public transportation is miserable. You can take the one-hour bus trip from Orvieto (the nearest train station) to Bagnoregio for $1 (3 buses run a day) or hitchhike. From Bagnoregio walk out of town past the gate, turn left at the pyramid monument and right at the first fork to get to the hotel. Without your own wheels it might make more sense to use Orvieto as a home base. It's a good transportation hub. The tourist office runs several good back-door-style day trips to nearby towns.

Tuscany, the province just to the north, also has some exciting

Day 14: Italian Hilltowns

hilltowns, many of which are served by trains and more frequent buses. Whatever you do, rip yourself out of the Venice-Florence-Rome syndrome. There's so much more to Italy. Give yourself a few days in Tuscany and Umbria. Seek out and savor its uncharted hilltowns. For starters, here's a map with a few of my favorites.

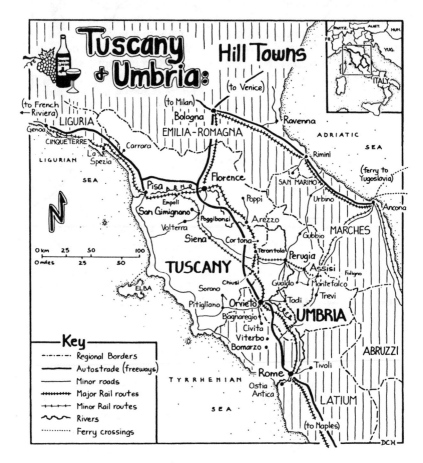

Day 15: Drive North to Pisa and the Italian Riviera

With breakfast and plenty of cappuccino under your belt, hit the autostrada and drive north for four hours, turning left at Florence, stopping at Pisa for lunch.

Pisa, a 30-minute drive out of the way, can be seen in about an hour. Its three important sights float regally in a lush green sea of grass — the best lawn I've seen in Italy, and ideal for a picnic. The Piazza of Miracles is the home of the famous Leaning Tower. The climb to the top is fun (294 tilted steps, open 8 am-7:30 pm). The huge cathedral (open 7:45 am-12:45 pm, 3 pm-6:45 pm) is actually more important artistically than the more famous tipsy tower. Finally, the Baptistry (same hours as church) is interesting for its great acoustics. The doorman uses its echo-power to actually sing haunting harmonies with himself.

One hour away is the port of La Spezia, where you'll park your car (hopefully at the station; otherwise, find a safe spot) and catch the 50-cent, 20-minute train ride into the Cinqueterre, Italy's Riviera wonderland.

Vernazza, one of five towns in the region, is the ideal home base, where, if you have called in advance, Sr. Sorriso will have dinner waiting. In the evening, wander down the main street (also the only street) to the harbor to join the visiting Italians in a sing-a-long. Have a gelato, cappuccino or glass of the local Cinqueterre wine in a waterfront cafe. Stay up as late as you like because tomorrow you can have a leisurely day.

Day 15: Suggested Schedule

8:00 am-12:00 pm Drive from Bagnoregio to Pisa.
12:00 pm- 2:00 pm Picnic lunch, sightsee, Pisa.
2:00 pm- 3:30 pm Drive to La Spezia.
3:30 pm- 4:00 pm Train to Vernazza.
　　　　　　　　　　Evening Free time in Vernazza.

Cinqueterre Train Schedule

Trains leaving La Spezia. A.M.: 1:15, 6:39, 7:20, 7:53, 9:05, 10:41, 11:21. P.M.: 12:22, 1:20, 2:33, 3:32, 5:00, 5:43, 6:16, 7:08, 7:41, 8:49, 10:47, 11:40.
Trains leaving Vernazza for La Spezia. A.M.: 12:28, 6:05, 6:58, 7:17, 8:44, 9:40, 10:56, 12:16, 1:36, 2:27, 3:38, 4:52, 5:35, 6:43, 7:05, 7:19, 8:46, 9:55, 10:42, 11:10.

All trains stop at each Cinqueterre town. On the map, towns #1, 2 & 3 are just a few minutes before or after Vernazza, town #4. These trains are in the "Locale" class (Italian for "milk run").

Food and Lodging

While Cinqueterre is unknown to the intenational mobs that ravage

Day 15: Pisa & the Italian Riviera

the Spanish and French coasts, plenty of Italians come here, so getting a room can be tough. August and weekends are bad. On weekends in August, forget it! But the area is worth planning ahead for.

In Vernazza, my favorite town, stay at Pension Sorriso (the only one in town), up the street from the station ($18 per person includes bed, breakfast and dinner, 19018 Vernazza, 5 Terre, La Spezia, tel. 0817-812224, English spoken. If that's full or too expensive Sr. Sorriso will help you find a private room.) It's easy to sleep free on the breakwater (check your bags at the station for 50 cents; showers on the beach; in the summer you'll have plenty of company).

In Riomaggiore, Hotel Argentina is above the town on Via di Gasperi #37. (tel. 0817-920213, $18 doubles, $25 triples). The restaurant in the center of town can usually find you a bed for $5.

In Manarola, Marina Piccola is located right on the water (tel. 0817-920103, around $10 per person).

When all else fails, you can stay in a noisy bigger town like La Spezia and take side trips into the villages.

Sorriso requires you take dinner from his pension; it's a forced luxury, and there is often fresh seafood. His house wine is great and, if you have an excuse to really celebrate, splurge on his strong, subtlely sweet and unforgettable Sciachetre wine.

Elsewhere, in Vernazza, the Castello (castle) restaurant serves great food just under the castle with Vernazza twinkling below you. The town's only gelati shop is excellent and most harborside bars will let you take your glass on a breakwater stroll.

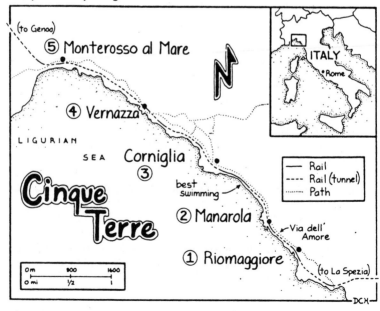

Day 16: A Vacation from Your Vacation: The Italian Riviera

Take a free day to enjoy the villages, swimming, hiking, sunshine, wine and evening romance of one of my favorite places anywhere. Pay attention to the schedules, and take advantage of the trains.

Helpful Hints

Pack your beach and swim gear, wear your walking shoes and catch the train to Riomaggiore. Walk the cliff-hanging Via dell' Amore to Manarola and buy food for a picnic and hike to Corniglia for the best beach around. There's a shower there, a bar and a cafe, which serves light food. The swimming is great and there's a train to zip you home later on. Or hike back to Vernazza.

If you're into *la dolce far niente* and don't want to hike, you could take the train directly to Corniglia to maximize beach time.

If you're a hiker, hike from Riomaggiore all the way to Monterosso al Mare, where a sandy "front-door-style" beach awaits. Pick a cactus fruit and ask a local to teach you how to peel it, *Delicioso!*

Each beach has showers that work better than your hotel's. Bring soap and shampoo. This is a good sunny time to wash clothes. When you get to Switzerland, your laundry won't dry as fast.

On your last night in Italy, be romantic. Sit on the breakwater, wine in hand, music in the background and let the warm waves lap at your feet.

Optional Itinerary

Hurried train travelers (who did the hilltowns on their way south) can take the train overnight to La Spezia from Rome, check their bags there, have 16 hours of fun in the Cinqueterre sun, and travel overnight again up to Switzerland. This would overcome the tricky hotel situation altogether. I haven't found anything nearly as nice as the Cinqueterre in this area so day tripping *from* this region makes no sense at all.

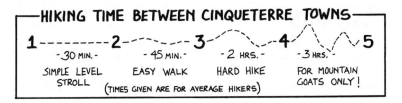

Day 17: From the Italian Riviera to the Alps

This is a long drive: scenic along the Mediterranean coast, boring during the stretch to Switzerland, and thrilling through the Alps.

Catch the 7 am train (skip Sorriso's breakfast; you'll hurt no one's feelings). If your car's where you left it, drive it on the autostrada along the stunning Riviera, skirting Christopher Columbus' home town of Genoa, noticing the crowded highrise living conditions of the Italy that most tourists choose to avoid, turning north through Italy's industrial heartland, past Milano with its hazy black halo and on into Switzerland. Just over the border is the Italian-speaking Swiss Riviera with famous resorts like Lugano and Locarno.

Bellinzona is a good town for a lunch break before climbing to the Alps. After driving through the Italian-speaking Swiss *canton* (state) of Ticino, famous for its ability to build just about anything out of stone, you'll take the longest tunnel in the world — the ten-mile-long Gotthard Pass Tunnel. It's so boring it's exciting. It hypnotizes most passengers into an open-jawed slumber until they pop out into the bright and cheery, green and rugged German-speaking Alpine world.

At Wassen (according to railroad buffs, the best place in Europe for train-watching) turn onto the Sustenpass road. Higher and higher you'll wind until you're at the snow-bound summit — a good place for a coffee stop. Give your intended hotel a call, toss a few snowballs, pop in your "Sound of Music" cassette and roll on.

Descend into the Bernese Oberland, rounding idyllic Lake Brienz to Interlaken. Stop for an hour here (park at the West Station) to take care of some administrative business. Banks abound. The one in the station is fair and stays open Monday through Saturday until 7 pm. A great tourist information office is just past the handy post office on the main street. Interlaken is the high class resort of the region, with the best shopping.

From Interlaken drive 30 minutes south into Lauterbrunnen (the name means "loud waterfalls") Valley, a glacier-cut cradle of Swissness. Park at the head of the valley in the gondola lot (safe and free). Ride the huge cable car straight up for five minutes ($2) to traffic-free Gimmelwald Village. A steep 100-yard climb uphill brings you to the chalet marked simply "Hotel." This is Walter Mittler's Hotel Mittaghorn; you have arrived.

Switzerland

16,000 square miles (one-fourth the size of Washington State).

6½ million people (400 per square mile, declining slightly).

Switzerland, Europe's richest, best-organized and most mountain-ous country, is an easy oasis and a breath of fresh Alpine air — much needed after intense Italy.

Not unlike the Boy Scouts, the Swiss count cleanliness, neatness, punctuality, tolerance, independence, thrift and hard work as virtues. They love the awesome nature that surrounds them and are proud of their many achievements. The average income of $14,270 (second highest in the world), a great social security system and their super-strong currency, not to mention the Alps, gives them plenty to be thankful for.

Switzerland, 60 percent of which is rugged Alps, has distinct cultural regions and customs. Two thirds of the people speak Ger-man, 20 per cent French, 10 per cent Italian, and a small group of people in the southeast speak Romansh, a direct descendant of ancient Latin. Within these four language groups, there are many dialects. An interest in these regional distinctions will win the hearts of locals you meet. As you travel from one valley to the next, notice changes in architecture and customs.

Historically, Switzerland is one of the oldest democracies. Born when three states, or *cantons*, united in 1291, the Confederation Helvetica as it's called (Roman name for the Swiss — notice "CH" on cars) grew, as our original 13 colonies did, to the 23 of today. The government is very decentralized and the canton is first on the Swiss citizen's list of loyalties.

Switzerland loves its neutrality, stayed out of both world wars, but is far from lax defensively. Every fit man serves in the army and stays in the reserve. Each house has a gun and a bomb shelter. With the push of a button, all road, rail and bridge entrances to the country can be destroyed, changing Switzerland into a formidable mountain fortress. August 1 is the Swiss national holiday.

Switzerland, because of its low inflation rate and the strength of the dollar, isn't as expensive as its reputation. Shops throughout the land thrill tourists with carved, woven and clanging mountain knick-knacks, clocks, watches, and Swiss army knives. (Remember, Victo-rinox is the best brand and the army uses the silver — not red — knives.)

The Swiss eat when we do and enjoy rather straightforward, no-nonsense cuisine, delicious fondue, rich chocolates, fresh dairy pro-ducts (try Muesli yogurt) and Fendant, a surprisingly good local white wine. The Co-op and Migros grocery stores are the hungry hiker's best budget bet.

Day 17 = To the Alps

You can get anywhere quickly on Switzerland's fine road system (the world's most expensive to build per mile), or on its scenic and efficient trains. Tourist information offices abound. While Switzerland's booming big cities are quite cosmopolitan, the traditional culture lives on in the Alpine villages. Spend most of your time high in the Alps. On Sundays you're most likely to enjoy traditional sports, music, clothing and culture.

Day 17: Suggested Schedule

7:00 am	Catch train.
7:30 am-12:30 pm	Drive freeway north to Switzerland.
12:30 pm- 1:30 pm	Lunch in Bellinzona or nearby town.
1:30 pm- 3:20 pm	Drive to Sustenpass, take a break.
3:40 pm- 6:30 pm	Drive to Interlaken, 1-hour stop, drive on to Stechelberg.
6:45 pm	Catch gondola to Gimmelwald, (last one: 7:30 pm).
7:00 pm	Learn why they say "If heaven isn't what it's cracked up to be, send me back to Gimmelwald."

Food and Lodging

While Switzerland bustles, Gimmelwald sleeps. It has a youth hostel, a pension, and a hotel. The hostel is simple, less than clean, rowdy, cheap ($2) and very friendly. It is often full, so call ahead to Lena, the elderly woman who runs the place (tel. 551704). The hostel has a self-serve kitchen and is one block from the lift station. Next-door is the pension with decent rooms and meals. Up the hill is the treasure of Gimmelwald: Walter Mittler, the perfect Swiss gentleman, who runs a chalet called Hotel Mittaghorn. It's a classic Alpine-style place with a million-dollar view of the Jungfrau Alps. Walter is careful not to get too hectic and big and enjoys sensitive, back-door travelers. He runs the hotel alone, keeping it simple, but with class. A former Swiss Air chef, his meals are the best around. He charges about $10 for bed and breakfast. (Address: 3801 Gimmelwald, Bern, Switzerland tel. 036-551658.)

Nearby towns have plenty of budget accommodations. Let each village's tourist office help you out.

Day 18: Alp Hike Day

If the weather is decent, you should set aside a day for hiking. The best hike is from Mannlichen to Kleine Scheidegg to Wengen. Get an early start, when the lifts are cheaper and the weather is usually better. Weather can change rapidly so always carry a sweater and raingear. Wear good walking shoes.

Recommended plan: Leave early. Ride lift to Murren, train to Grutschalp, funicular to Lauterbrunnen, cross the street and catch the train to Wengen. Do any necessary banking or picnic shopping. Catch cable car to Mannlichen. Hike to little peak for grand view, then walk (one hour) around to Kleine Scheidegg for lunch. There are a few restaurants or you can picnic.

If you've got an extra $30 and the weather is perfect ride the train through the Eiger to the towering Jungfraujoch and back. From Kleine Scheidegg, enjoy the ever-changing Alpine panorama of the North Face of the Eiger, Jungfrau and Moench, probably accompanied by the valley-filling mellow sound of alp horns, as you hike gradually downhill (2 hours) to the town of Wengen. If the weather turns bad or you run out of steam, you can catch the train earlier. The trail is very good and the hike is easy for any fit person.

Wengen is a fine shopping town. Catch the train from Wengen to Lauterbrunnen to avoid the steep and boring final descent. Ride back up to Grutschalp, take the train or hike to Murren, and walk back

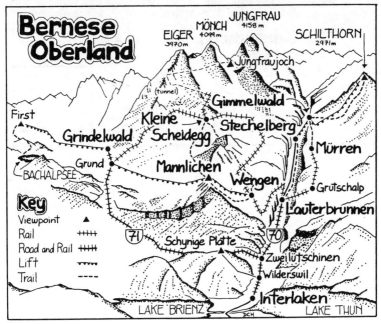

down to Hotel Mittaghorn (45 minutes). Total cost of today's lifts —
around $20.

Evening fun in Gimmelwald is found in the hostel (lots of young
Alp-happy hikers and a good chance to share information on the
surrounding mountains), in the pension dining room (hearty soup,
cheap beer, social gathering spot for locals and hostelers), and up at
Walter's. If Walter is serving dinner, don't miss it. Be sure to try his
Kaffe-fertig which has a cult following among my tour groups. Sit on
his porch, watch the sun lick the mountain tops to bed and the moon
rise over the Jungfrau.

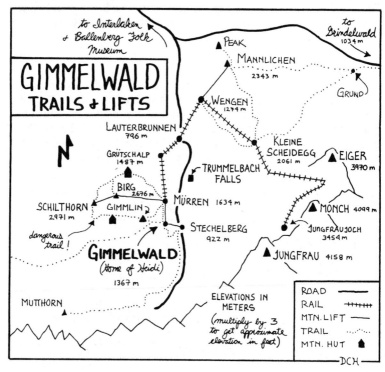

Day 19: Free Time in the Alps, Evening Drive into France

If the weather's good, take another hike. The Schilthorn offers the most Alpine excitement around. Late in the afternoon it's time to move on, driving out of the Alps and into France's Alsace region to Colmar — a whole new world.

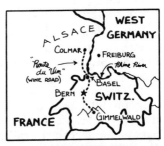

Helpful Hints

Walter serves a great breakfast, but if the weather's good, skip his and eat on top of the Schilthorn, at 10,000 feet, in a slowly revolving mountain-capping restaurant (of James Bond movie fame). The early gondola ride (7:30 am or 7:50 am) is discounted enough to pay for your ham and eggs. Try the *Birchermuesli*-yogurt treat.

For hikers: The gondola (Gimmelwald-Schilthorn-Gimmelwald) ride costs about $20. The hike (G-S-G) is free, if you don't mind a 5,000-foot altitude gain. I ride up and hike down or, for a less scary hike, go up and half way down by cable car and walk down from the Birg station. Lifts go twice an hour and the ride takes 30 minutes. (The round-trip excursion early-bird fare is cheaper than Gimmelwald-Schilthorn-Birg. If you buy that ticket you can decide at Birg if you want to hike or ride down.) Linger on top. Watch hang gliders set up, psych up and take off, flying 30 or 40 minutes with the birds to distant Interlaken. Walk along the ridge out back. You can even convince yourself you climbed to that perch and feel pretty rugged. Think twice before descending from the Schilthorn (weather can change, have good shoes). Most people would have more fun hiking from Birg. Just below Birg is a mountain hut. Drop in for soup, cocoa, or a coffee-schnapps. You can spend the night for $5.

The most interesting trail from Murren to Gimmelwald is the high one via Gimmlin. Murren has plenty of shops, bakeries, tourist, information, bank, a modern sports complex...

Itinerary Options

If the weather is bad, or you happen to hate mountains, try this: The Lauterbrunnen-Interlaken train ($2, 30 minutes, goes frequently) will zip you into the big town resort of the region. Interlaken has lots of resorty activities and shopping. At the other end of Lake Brienz is Switzerland's best open-air folk museum: Ballenberg (open 9 am-5:30 pm daily). It's the best possible look at Swiss folk life, with old traditional buildings from all over the country gathered together displaying the old culture.

Day 19: To France

Transportation

If you are traveling by car, by 4 pm you should be speeding out of the mountains, past the Swiss capital of Bern and on towards Basel, where Switzerland snuggles against both Germany and France.

Before Basel you'll go through a tunnel and come to a strange, orange structure that looks like a huge submarine laying eggs on the freeway. Stop here for dinner and a look around one of Europe's greatest freeway rest stops. There's a bakery and grocery store for picnickers and a restaurant. Spend some time goofing around, then carry on (Interlaken to Colmar is a 4-hour drive). From Basel follow the signs to France. In France head north to Colmar, where you can park on the huge square called Place Rapp, and check into the nearby Hotel Rapp. Wander around the old town (Tanner's Quarters), have a dessert crêpe, or taste some local wine.

For train travelers, the Eurailpass won't work on the mountain lines south of Interlaken. Upon arrival in Interlaken ask about the Jungfrau Region trains — schedules, prices and special deals. Also, lay the groundwork for your departure by getting the Interlaken-Colmar schedule. It's a very easy trip. From the Colmar station you can walk to Hotel Rapp, about 10 minutes.

Optional Itinerary

From the Cinqueterre you could trade Switzerland for France and spend a day in Nice, Cannes and Monte Carlo. Take the night train to Chamonix for the best of the French Alps (Mont Blanc) and take the night-train (12 am-8 pm) directly into Paris from there. This plan is much better by train than by car.

From Interlaken you can also do minor surgery on your itinerary, skip Alsace entirely, and go directly to Paris (excellent overnight train or all-day drive).

If you're not really interested in France it would be interesting to mosey back to Amsterdam via more of Switzerland, the Bodensee, the Black Forest, Trier, Mosel Valley, Luxembourg, Brussels and Bruges. This is mostly small-town and countryside travel so it's best for car travelers.

Or, you may decide to sell your plane ticket and permanently join Heidi and the cows waiting for eternity in Europe's greatest cathedral — the Swiss Alps.

France

210,000 square miles (Europe's largest country, Texas-sized).
55 million people (248 per square mile, 78 percent urban).

You may have heard that the French are mean and cold. Don't believe it. If anything, they're pouting because they're no longer the world's premier culture. It's tough to be crushed by a Big Mac and keep on smiling. Be sensitive and understanding. The French are cold only if you choose to perceive them that way. Look for friendliness, give people the benefit of the doubt, respect all that's French and you'll remember France with a smile.

Formerly the world's most powerful country, France has much to offer in so many ways. Paris will overwhelm you if you don't do a little studying. And Paris is just the beginning of Europe's largest and most diverse country.

Learn some French — at least the polite words — and try to sound like Maurice Chevalier. The French don't speak much English — but they speak much more English than we speak French. Unless you speak French, you'll have to be patient about any communications problems.

The French are experts in the art of fine living. Their cuisine, their customs, even their vacationing habits, are highly developed. Since the vacation is such a big part of the French lifestyle (nearly every worker takes either July or August off), you'll find no shortage of tourist information centers, hotels, transportation facilities and fun ways to pass free days.

The French eat lunch from 12 pm-2 pm, dinner from 7 pm-10 pm — and eat well. Each region has its high cuisine specialties and even the "low cuisine" of a picnic can be elegant, with fresh bread and an endless variety of tasty French cheeses, meats, rich pastries and, of course, wine. The best approach to French food is to eat where locals eat and be adventurous. Eat ugly things with relish!

The French government takes pride in its independence from the USA, USSR, Britain, Germany, and the Church. While the French per capita income is a respectable $10,650, and while the nation leads Europe in farm production, France's economy under its socialist government has gone very flat. France has a large poor class (the poorest 20 per cent of the people have only 2 percent of the wealth) and the French franc has sunk to record lows. A few years ago there were four francs to a dollar. At the time of this writing there are nine.

With the U.S. dollar so strong, France is not only a cheap place to travel (plenty of $15 double rooms) but a shopper's delight. Visitors are consistently lured away from important sights by important savings on luxury items, high fashions, perfume, antiques and tourist trinkets, ranging from glow-in-the-dark necklaces to fake gargoyles.

Food and Lodging

In general, France is wonderful for the budget traveler. Any one-star or two-star hotel (indicated by a blue-and-white plaque near the door) will offer bed and breakfast for $5 to $10 per person. Popular Colmar and Alsace can be difficult in peak season so, as usual, it's wise to arrive early or call ahead. Hotel Rapp in Colmar is ideal. Friendly, intimate, with a great local restaurant, $12 doubles, English spoken. It's run by Bernard, who mixes class with warmth like no man I've met. If he's full, ask him for a recommendation. Hotel Turenne (10 Rt. de Bale, tel. 89-411226) is next best. The tourist information office can also find you a room. Nearby towns and villages aren't so crowded and can offer an even more Alsacian hotel experience. But Colmar is your best headquarters town.

Alsacian cuisine is a major tourist attraction in itself. Bernard's restaurant in Hotel Rapp is my dress-up, high-cuisine splurge of the tour ($10). I comb my hair, change my socks and savor a slow, elegant meal served with grace and fine wine. Why not? Don't miss the "Rapp salad."

Day 20: Colmar, Alsacian Villages, Wine Tasting

After a Bernard breakfast, spend the morning exploring Colmar. After a late lunch at Flunch (a great French self-serve cafeteria chain) go into the countryside to wander the *Route du Vin* (wine road) and visit the villages of Eguisheim and Kayserberg. Drop by a winery for a tour and tasting before returning to Hotel Rapp for dinner.

Helpful Hints

The old town is easily covered on foot. Worthwhile guidebooks are in most gift shops and the tourist office can provide maps, hours and general information and ideas for your trip into the wine road region.

Sightseeing Highlights

*** **Unterlinden Museum** — Colmar's touristic claim to fame, this is one of my favorite museums in Europe. While its collection ranges from Roman Colmar to medieval wine-making exhibits to traditional wedding dresses to babies' cribs to Picasso, Grunewald's gripping Isenheim Altarpiece deserves top billing. Pick

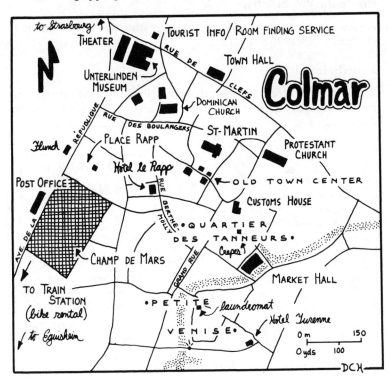

up the English guidebook at the desk, study the polyptic model of the multi-paneled painting on the wall next to the original, and get acquainted with this greatest of late-medieval German masterpieces.

** **Dominican Church** — This is another medieval mind-blower that awaits your attention. In the Dominican church you'll find Martin Schongauer's angelically beautiful *Madonna of the Roses,* looking like it was painted yesterday, holding court on center stage (open 10 am-5 pm).

Tanner's Quarters — This refurbished chunk of the old town is a delight, day or night.

Bartholdi Museum — A mediocre but interesting little museum about the life and work of the local boy who gained fame by sculpting our Statue of Liberty. You'll notice several of his statues, usually with one arm raised high, gracing Colmar's Squares.

Colmar is a good place for mailing things. (Paris is a headache). The post office near Place Rapp sells boxes, is open 8 am-7 pm, and is a good place to lighten your load. Colmar is also a good place to do laundry and to shop (stores close Monday mornings).

Route du Vin Sidetrip

Alsace has so much to offer. If you have only one afternoon, limit yourself to these two towns:

Eguisheim

Just a few miles from Colmar, this scenic little town is best explored by walking around its circular road, then cutting through the middle.

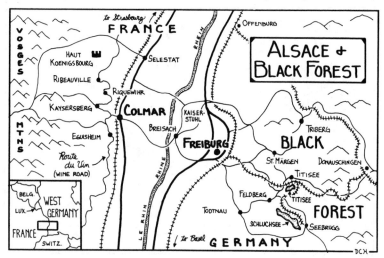

Visit the Eguisheim Wine Cooperative. You may have to wait for a group to enjoy their free tour and tasting. (The French words for hangover — if you get really "Alsaced" — *Mal à la tête.*)

Kaysersberg

Albert Schweitzer's hometown is larger but just as cute as Eguisheim. Climb the castle, browse through the art galleries, taste some wine (*degustation* means "come on in and taste") and wander along nearby vineyards.

By car this is easy. Otherwise buses are possible, but I'd recommend renting a bike at the Colmar station for your wine road excursion (go easy on the tasting).

Day 20: Suggested Schedule

8:00 am	Breakfast.
8:30 am	Orientation walk, ending at tourist office.
9:00 am-10:30 am	Unterlinden Museum.
10:30 am- 1:00 pm	Free time to shop, sightsee, wash or mail.
1:00 pm	Lunch at Flunch.
2:00 pm- 6:00 pm	Exploration of wine road and villages.
7:30 pm	Dinner, Hotel Rapp

Day 21: The Long Drive to Paris, Stopping at Reims

A day's journey will take you halfway across France to Paris, with a stop for lunch, a champagne tour and a visit to the great Gothic cathedral in Reims. You'll be in Paris in time for dinner, a subway lesson and a city orientation tour.

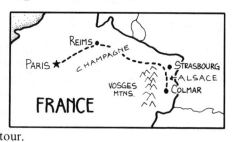

Reims

The cathedral of Reims is one of the best examples of Gothic architecture you'll see. Its front end is considered the best west portal anywhere, and for 800 years it was the coronation place of French kings and queens. It houses many old treasures, not to mention a lovely set of Marc Chagall stained glass windows. Take this opportunity to fall in love with Gothic. (Open 8 am to 9 pm daily.)

Reims is the capital of the Champagne region and, while the bubbly stuff's birthplace was Epernay, it's best to save nearly two hours of road time by touring a Champagne cave right in Reims. Walk 10 mintues up Rue de Barbatre from the Cathedral to #9 Place S. Nicaise (tel. 85-4535) where the Tattinger Company will do a great job trying to convince you they're the best. After seeing their movie (the comfy theater seats alone make this a worthwhile visit), follow your guide down into some of the three miles of chilly chalk caves, many dug by ancient Romans. Popping corks signal when the tour's done and the tasting's begun.

One block beyond Tattinger, on Place des Droits de l'Homme, you'll find several other Champagne firms. Most give free tours from 2 pm to 5 pm. I'd recommend Piper Heidsieck (51 Blvd. Henry-Vasnier, tel. 85-0194) and Veuve Clicquot-Pousardin (#1 Place des Droits de l'Homme, tel. 85-2568). If you want to drive to Epernay (nice town, plenty of cheap hotels) the best Champagne firm with the best tours is right downtown — Moët Chandon.

Transportation

Drivers should leave Colmar by 7:30 am, head north past Strasbourg and take the autobahn straight to Reims (5 hours). You'll pass Verdun (an interesting stop for history and WWI buffs) and lots of strange (even silly) modern Franco-freeway art.

Take the Reims exit marked "Cathedral" and you'll see your destination. Park near the church. Picnic in the park near its front (public wc, dangerous grass, glorious setting).

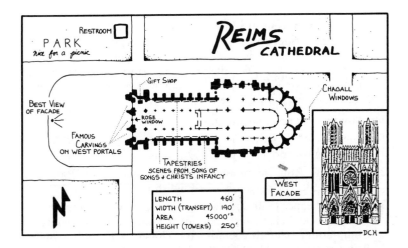

Back on the freeway, it's a straight shot (excepting toll booth stops) into Paris. By this schedule, you should hit it just about rush hour (No tour is perfect).

If you're renting a car it would be handy, if possible, to turn it in at the Charles de Gaulle airport and take the bus or subway into town. Or call your hotel from Reims and ask if you can arrive late. Or just damn the torpedoes, think of it as San Francisco or Boston, fasten your seatbelt, check your insurance, and drive. If you're in danger of going "in-Seine," hire a cab and follow him to your hotel. If you think you're good behind the wheel, drive this introductory tour as the sun sets: go over the Austerlitz Bridge, to the Luxembourg Gardens, down Boulevard St. Michel, past Notre Dame on the island, up Rue du Rivoli, past the Louvre, through the Place de la Concorde, up the Champs-Elysees, around the Arc de Triomphe (6 or 8 giggly times) and to your hotel. (Confirm your hotel reservation upon arrival or earlier in the day by telephone.)

By train you can connect from Colmar to Reims to Paris easily, but I'd probably skip Reims, save a day, and take the train overnight direct to Paris. Chartres Cathedral, an hour's side trip from Paris is as good as Reims.

NOTE: Please don't skip Paris. If Europe is a shoe, Paris is the laces.

Food and Lodging

Paris will only give you trouble in May and September, or if you look for beds in the shadow of famous buildings. (Don't look around the Eiffel Tower.) Take the subway to any neighborhood that you've never heard of, walk down the street, and find your own special one- or two-star (blue-and-white plaque) hotel offering beds with a smile for $10 or less each.

Day 21: To Reims & Paris

A handy, quiet, central and reasonably safe neighborhood with a cluster of fine budget hotels is at the Metro (subway) stop, Montmartre (in the ninth district, halfway between the Opera and the Pompidou Center). Find the quiet alley running between rue Bergère and Boulevard Poissonnière (30 yards in front of the Flunch — yippee! — and through a corridor on the left).

My Montmartre recommendations:

1. Hotel des Arts (7 Cité Bergère, 75009 Paris. tel. 246-7330, $25 dbls., English spoken, friendly.)
2. Hotel Cite Rougemont (4 Cite Rougemont, 75009 Paris. tel. 770-2595 $12 per person, some English.)
3. Several cheaper ($20 doubles, not so clean, very acceptable — cleanliness and character often ride the same teeter-totter): Hotel Comprador (2 Cité Rougemont, tel. 770-4442); Hotel Rex (4 Cite Rougemont, tel. 824-6070); Hotel d'Espagne (9 Cité Bergère, tel. 770-1394).

Other areas:

Hotel de Douai (32 rue de Douai, 75009 Paris, tel. 874-4867). People love it or hate it. Bubbles with character on edge of red light district and seedy side roads. One block from Moulin Rouge (Metro stop: Blanche). $15-20 doubles. Jane, the night-watch lady, writes upside down and will happily talk your ears off, especially if you are interested in the Celtic struggles of Brittany. Hotel Daguerre (94 Rue Daguerre, 75014 Paris, tel. 322-4354, near Metro stop: Guite, off Ave du Marne) is cheap, comfy, English-speaking, and is a great locale, near Montparnasse Tower.

You could eat yourself silly in Paris. The city could hold a gourmet's Olympics — and import nothing. I picnic or self-serve it for quick lunches and linger longer over delicious dinners. You can eat very well, restaurant style, for $6 or $8. Ask your hotel to recommend a small, French restaurant nearby in the 50 to 100-franc range. Famous places are overpriced, overcrowded and usually overrated. Find a quiet neighborhood and wander or follow a local recommendation. You'll dine fine.

Self-serve recommendations: There are plenty. Check department store top floors (Samartine at Pont Neuf near Louvre). Flunch has branches near all the hotels I recommended (just coincidence), and on Champs-Elysées.

Small, family-style Parisian restaurant favorites: La Petite Bouclerie (33 rue de la Harpe, in Latin Quarter). This has family cooking with class on busy, fun, if over-touristed street $7-10. Au Fleuri (51 rue Blanche, down the street from recommended Hotel de Douai) is very local-style with self-service prices.

British Isles

Sample Tour by Car

Day

1 Arrive London, pick-up car, Brighton, Winchester

2 Winchester, Salisbury, Stonehenge, Bath

3 Bath. Walking tour of city, Roman Baths, Museum of Costume

4 Bath, Cotswold Villages, Stow-on-the Wold for two nights

5 More in the Cotswolds. . .explore the land of "Quaint"

6 Cotswolds, Stratford-on-Avon, North Wales

7 Wales, a whole new culture, castles, villages, mountains

8 North Wales, Snowdon National Park, Chester

9 Windemere Lakes District

10 Hadrian's Wall, Roman Museum, Edinburgh

Day

11 Edinburgh, entire day to sightsee, explore and shop

12 Drive south to York, walking tour, great shopping

13 York, medieval streets, York Minster, Castle Museum

14 Cambridge, historic colleges, walking tour*

15 London, mid-day introduction tour, evening play

16 London, plenty of sightseeing, trip-end party

17 London, more sightseeing, tour over. Return home or ?

*Drop car at Cambridge if possible on day 14 and train into London or drop car back at airport on day 15.

Spain-Portugal-Morocco
Sample Tour by Car

Day

1 Sightsee Lisbon, Portugal's capital. Plenty to do: the salty sailors' quarter, the Alfama, historic museums, evening at the Faire Populare. Possibly a Fado performance.

2 Lisbon, Sintra, Cascais, Estoril

3 Obidos, Batalha, Nazare. Explore ruined Moorish castle, perfect medieval walled-town and fishing village.

4 Drive inland, Portuguese countryside, many cultural thrills per minute, mile and dollar.

5 Evora

6 Leave early, drive south cross-country to South coast, Algarve, sunny beaches and white-washed houses

7 Free day on Algarve. Salema—best beach town, near Lagos

8 More Algarve, a whole day for vigorous relaxation on the beach or in the villages.

9 Drive early to Spain. Lunch and afternoon in Seville, plenty to see, the famous Alcazar, Jewish and Gypsie quarter.

Day

10 Explore small Spanish towns. Estepa

11 Ronda, prehistoric Pileta Cave paintings (drawing done 25,000 years ago!)

12 Boat to Morocco. Drive south.

13 Market Day in Chechaouen. Afternoon drive to Fes.

14 All day free to explore Fes.

15 Volubilis, Roman city ruins. Moulay-Idriss, Holy city-market day.

16 Fes, drive north back to Chechaouen.

17 Boat to Spain

18 Costa del Sol

19 Granada, tour the last Moorish palace/ stronghold, the Alhambra, and the Gypsie quarters, Sacromonte.

20 Drive north to Toledo.

21 Madrid. All day sightsee, the great Prado museum, Royal Palace and Plaza Mayor.

Scandinavia
Sample Tour by Car

Day

1 Fly to Copenhagen.
2 Arrive at Copenhagen airport. Set up, orientation, relax
3 Copenhagen city sights, palace, shopping, evening at Tivoli
4 North Zealand, Frederiksborg Castle, Kronborg (Hamlet) Castle, Louisiana ultra-modern art museum, boats to Sweden. Evening in Lund.
5 Drive from Lund to Stockholm. Stockholm orientation.
6 Stockholm city sights—Gamla Stan, Royal Palace, Historic center, smorgasbord midday feast, sauna
7 Stockholm—Millesgarten, Wasa, Skansen Swedish Openair Folk Museum. Evening fun at Skansen and Grona Lund amusement park.
8 Explore Uppsala—historic capitol and university town. Dalarna where the Swedish

Day

folk cultures mixes so comfortably with the beautiful natural scenery.
9 Drive to Oslo, downtown sightseeing tour..
10 Oslo—city sights—boat to Bygdoy for open-air folk museum, Kon-Tiki, Ra, Fram and the best Viking ships anywhere.
11 Villages and Interior of Norway.
12 Interior and fjords of West Norway.
13 Bergen, historic and trading capitol.
14 Bergen, medieval stavechurch, Troldhaug fjord country.
15 Fjord country, Setesdal Valley.
16 Setesdal—South Norway.
17 South Coast.
18 Boat to Jutland, Denmark.
19 Odense, Hans Christian Anderson Land.
20 Free day to be used anywhere on the tour.
21 Roskilde to Copenhagen.
22 Copenhagen, tour over, fly home when you like.

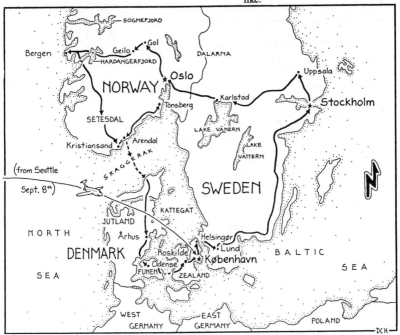

Greece-Yugoslavia
Sample Tour by Car

Day

1 Fly USA-Athens. Hotel in Plaka.
2 Athens—Plaka, Agora, Acropolis, evening dine and dance in Plaka.
3 Athens—National Museum, pick up car, drive over Corinth Canal to Nafplion.
4 Nafplion—Morning—ruins of Mycenae. Afternoon—Epidavros Theater. Evening—seafood on Nafplion waterfront.
5 Nafplion—Sparta (lunch), Mystra—Byzantine ruins, Jerolimin—tiny coastal village.
6 Jerolimin—Pirgos Dirous caves—Koroni
7 Koroni—Finikous, remote fishing village, great beach.
8 Finikous—drive north, explore Olympia ruins.
9 Long drive to Olympia—Rion ferry—Ionnina—Metsovo.
10 Metsovo—colorful Romanian town, good shopping. Meteora—pinnacle monasteries. Enchanting.
11 Meteora—Ohrid, Yugoslavia. Mysterious

Day

town on border of Albania. "Sobe" = bed and breakfast in Yugoslavian.
12 Ohrid—Prizen. This is a Muslim-Albanian world about as "un-western" as is possible in Europe.
13 Prizren—Pec. Make things happen here. The people are great.
14 Pec—Cetinje, the historic capital of rugged Montenegro.
15 Cetinje—Dubrovnik, stay in "sobe." Don't miss the folk dancing at the Revelin Fort.
16 Dubrovnik. A free day for Europe's most romantic city.
17 Dubrovnik—Korcula. A mini-Dubrovnik on an island.
18 Korcula—Mostar—Sarajevo. A giant busy city with a fascinating old town.
19 Sarajevo—sightsee in the morning and drive through winding mountain roads to Titovo that evening.
20 Titovo—south by autobahn to any coastal town off freeway near Mt. Olympus.

European Weather

Here is a list of average temperatures and days of no rain. This can be helpful in planning your itinerary, but I have never found European weather to be particularly predictable.

1st line: ave. daily low; 2nd: ave. daily high; 3rd: days of no rain

	J	F	M	A	M	J	J	A	S	O	N	D
FRANCE Paris	32°	34°	36°	41°	47°	52°	55°	55°	50°	44°	38°	33°
	42°	45°	52°	60°	67°	73°	76°	75°	69°	59°	49°	43°
	16	15	16	16	18	19	19	19	19	17	15	14
GERMANY Frankfurt	29°	31°	35°	41°	48°	53°	56°	55°	51°	43°	36°	31°
	37°	42°	49°	58°	67°	72°	75°	74°	67°	56°	45°	39°
	22	19	22	21	22	21	21	21	21	22	21	20
GREAT BRITAIN London	35°	35°	37°	40°	45°	51°	55°	54°	51°	44°	39°	36°
	44°	45°	51°	56°	63°	69°	73°	72°	67°	58°	49°	45°
	14	15	20	16	18	19	18	18	17	17	14	15
ITALY Rome	39°	39°	42°	46°	55°	60°	64°	64°	61°	53°	46°	41°
	54°	56°	62°	68°	74°	82°	88°	88°	83°	73°	63°	56°
	23	17	26	24	25	28	29	28	24	22	22	22
NETHERLANDS Amsterdam	34°	34°	37°	43°	50°	55°	59°	59°	56°	48°	41°	35°
	40°	41°	46°	52°	60°	65°	69°	68°	64°	56°	47°	41°
	12	13	18	16	19	18	17	17	15	13	11	12
SWITZERLAND Geneva	29°	30°	35°	41°	48°	55°	58°	57°	52°	44°	37°	31°
	39°	43°	51°	58°	66°	73°	77°	76°	69°	58°	47°	40°
	20	19	21	19	19	19	22	21	20	20	19	21

European Festivals

Each country has a "4th of July" celebration. A visit to a country during its national holiday can only make your stay more enjoyable.

Austria	Oct. 26	Netherlands	April 30
France	July 14	Switzerland	Aug. 1
Italy	June 2	West Germany	June 17

EUROPEAN FESTIVALS

Austria
Salzburg Festival, July 26-Aug 30. Greatest musical festival, focus on Mozart

England
Jousting Tournament of Knights, last Sun & Mon in May at Chilham Castle near Canterbury. Medieval pageantry, colorful.

Allington Castle Medieval Market, 2nd or 3rd Sat in June in Maidstone (30 mi SE London). Medieval crafts and entertainment.

Druid Summer Solstice Ceremonies, June 20 or 21. Stonehenge, Hoods and white robes, rituals from midnight to sunrise at about 4:45 a.m.

Ainwick Medieval Fair, last Sun in June to next Sat. Medieval costumes, competition, entertainment. Ainwick, 30 mi N of Newscastle.

Haslemere Early Music Festival, 2 Fridays before 4th Sat in July. 16th-18th c. music on original instruments. 40 mi S of London.

Sidmouth Int'l Folklore Festival, 1st to 2nd Fridays of August, 300 events, 15 mi E of Exeter.

Reading Rock Festival, last weekend in August. England's best. 40 mi W of London.

Nottingham Goose Fair, 1st Thurs-Sat in Oct, one of England's oldest and largest fairs. Nottingham.

Guy Fawkes Day, Nov. 5. Nationwide holiday.

France
Fetes de la St. Jean, around June 24, 3 days of folklore and bull running in streets. St. Jean de Luz (on coast, S or Bordeaux).

Tour de France, first 3 weeks of July, 2,000 mile bike race around France ending in Paris.

Maubeuge Int'l Beer Festival, Thursday before July 14 for two weeks. Great entertainment and beer in largest beer tent. In Maubeuge near Belgian border.

Bastille Day, July 13 & 14. Great National Holiday all over France. Paris has biggest festivities.

Great Festival of Corouaille, 4th Sun in July. Huge Celtic folk festival at Quimper in Brittany.

Alsace Wine Fair, 2nd & 3rd weekends in Aug in Colmar.

Festival of Minstrels, 1st Sun in Sept. Wine, music, folklore, etc. in Ribeauville 35 mi S of Strasbourg.

Fete d'Humanite, 2nd or 3rd Sat and Sun of September. Huge communist fair color festivities — not all red. Paris.

Germany
Der Meistertrunk, Sat before Whit Monday. Music, dancing, beer, sausage in Rothenburg o.d.T.

Pied Piper's Procession, Sundays, 1:00 p.m. all summer, Hamlin (where else?).

Ayinger Volksfest, 2nd thru 3rd weekend in June. White bear, concerts and Maypole dancing at Aying, 15 mi SE of Munich.

Freiburger Weinfest, last Fri thru following Tuesday in June. Wine festival in Black Forest town of Freiburg.

Kinderzeche, weekend before 3rd Mon in July to weekend after. Festival honoring children who saved town in 1640's. Dinkelsbuhl.

Trier Weinfest, Sat to 1st Mon in Aug. Trier.

Gaubondenfest, 2nd Fri in Aug for 10 days. 2nd only to Oktoberfest. Straubing 25 mi SE of Regensburg.

Der Rhein in Flammen, 2nd Sat in Aug. Dancing, wine and beer festivals, bonfires. Koblenz to Braubach.

Moselfest, last weekend in Aug or 1st in Sept. Mosel wine festival in Winningen.

Backfischfest, last Sat in Aug for 15 days. Largest wine and folk festival on the Rhine in Worms.

Wurstmarkt, 2nd Sat, Sept, through following Tuesday. And 3rd Fri through following Monday. World's largest wine festival in Bad Durkheim, 25 mi W of Heidelberg.

Oktoberfest, starting 3rd to last Sat in Sept through 1st Sun in Oct. World's most famous beer festival, Munich.

Italy

Sagra del Pesche, 2nd Sunday in May. One of Italy's great popular events, huge feast of freshly caught fish, fried in world's largest pans. Camogli, 10 mi S of Genoa.

Festa de Ceri, May 15. One of the world's most famous folklore events, colorful pageant, giant feast afterwards. Gubbio, in hill country, 25 mi NE of Perugia.

"Palio of the Archers," last Sun of May. Re-enactment of medieval crossbow contest with arms and costumes. Gubbio, 130 mi NE of Rome.

"Palio," July 2 and Aug 16. Horse race which is Italy's most spectacular folklore event. Medieval procession beforehand. 35,000 spectators. Siena, 40 mi SW of Florence.

Joust of the Saracen, 1st Sun of Sept. Costumed equestrian tournament dating from 13th c. Crusades against the Muslim Saracens. Arezzo, 40 mi SE of Florence.

Historical Regatta, 1st Sun of Sept. Gala procession of decorated boats followed by double-oared gondola race. Venice.

Human Chess Game, 1st or 2nd weekend in Sept on even-numbered years. Medieval pageantry and splendor accompany re-enactment of human chess game in 1454. Basso Castle in Marostica, 40 mi NW of Venice.

Netherlands

Kaasmarkt, Fridays only from late April to late Sept. Colorful cheese market with members of 350 yr old Cheese Carriers' Guild. Alkmaar, 15 mi N of Amsterdam.

North Sea Jazz Festival, weekend of 3rd Sun in July. World's greatest jazz weekend. 100 concerts with 500+ musicians. Den Haag.

Switzerland

Landsgemeinde, 1st Sun in May. Largest open-air parliamentary session. Glarus, 40 mi SE of Zurich.

Montreux International Jazz Festival, 1st through 3rd weekends in July. Comprehensive annual musical events featuring top artists. Montreux.

William Tell Plays, 2nd Thurs in July through 1st Sun in Sept. Dramatic presenta-

These are just a few of Europe's countless folk and music festivals. Each country's National Tourist Office in the USA will send you a free calendar of events. The best book I've seen for a listing of the great festivals of Europe is Playboy's *Guide to Good Times: Europe*, $2.95. ISBN 0-872-16819-0.

Foreign Phrases

Practical Foreign Phrases

DUTCH

1.	Hello	Goedemiddag	Goo-der-mid-dahkh
2.	Goodbye	Tot ziens	Tot seenss
3.	Please	Alstublieft	Ahls-stew-bleeft
4.	Thank you	Dank U	Dahngk ew
5.	One	Een	Any
6.	Two	Twee	Tvay
7.	Three	Drie	Dree
8.	Four	Vier	Veer
9.	Five	Vijf	Vayf
10.	Six	Zes	Zehss
11.	Seven	Zeven	Zay-vern
12.	Eight	Acht	Ahkht
13.	Nine	Negen	Nay-gern
14.	Ten	Tien	Teen
15.	Twenty	Twintig	Tvin-tich
16.	Fifty	Vijftig	Vayf-tich
17.	One Hundred	Honderd	Hon-derrt
18.	Yes	Ja	Yar
19.	No	Nee	Nay
20.	Cheap/Expensive	Goedkoop/Duur	Goot-koap/Dewr
21.	Cheers	Proost!	Proast!
22.	Beautiful	Mooi	Moaee
23.	Delicious	Uitstekende	Oit-stay-kun-duh
24.	What do you call this?	Hoe noemt u dat?	Hoo noomt ew daht?
25.	I don't understand	Ik begrijp het niet	Ik ber-grayp-heht neet
26.	How are you?	Hoe gaat het?	Hoo gart hurt?
27.	Excuse me	Neemt u me niet kwalijk	Naymt ew mer neet kvarlerk
28.	Very	Zeer	Zayr
29.	Good/bad	Goed/slecht	Goot/slehkht
30.	Big/small	Groot/klein	Groat/klayn
31.	Fast/slow	Snel/langzaam	Snehl/lahngzarm
32.	Where is?	Waar is?	Wahr is?
33.	How much?	Hoeveel?	Hoo vill?
34.	friend	vriend	vrent
35.	toilet	wc	vay say
36.	water	water	water

GERMAN

1. hello	guten tag	goo-ten tock
2. goodbye	auf wiedersehn	awf VEE-der-sayn
3. see you later	bis spater	beess SHPAY-tuh
4. goodnight	gute nacht	GOO-tuh nahkt
5. please	bitte	BIT-teh
6. thank you	danke schon	DONG-kuh shayn
7. yes/no	ja/nein	yah/nine
8. one/two/three	eins/zwei/drei	aintz/tzvy/dry
9. cheap/expensive	billig/teuer	BIL-ikh/TOY-err
10. good/bad	gut/schlecht	goot/shlehkht
11. beautiful/ugly	schon/hasslich	shurn/HESS-leek
12. big/small	gross/klein	groass/kline
13. fast/slow	schnell/langsam	shnel/LONG-zahm
14. very	sehr	zair
15. where is . . . ?	wo ist . . . ?	voh ist
16. how much . . . ?	wieviel	vee-FEEL
17. I don't understand	ich verstehe nicht	ikh vehr-SHTAY-er nicht
18. what do you call this?	wie heisst das?	vee HEIST dahss
19. I'm lost	ich habe mich verirrt	ikh hah-beh mikh fehr-IRT
20. complete price (everything included)	alles ist inbegriffen	AHlerss ist IN-ber-grif-ern
21. I'm tired	ich bin mude	ikh bin MEW-duh
22. I'm hungry	ich habe hunger	ikh hah-beh HOONG-guh
23. cheers!	prosit!	proast
24. food	speise	SHPY-zuh
25. grocery store	laden	LODD-en
26. picnic	picknick	pik-nik
27. delicious	lecker	LECK-uh
28. market	markt	markt
29. drunk	betrunken	beh-TROHN-ken
30. money	geld	gelt
31. station	bahnhof	BAHN-hof
32. private accommodations	zimmer	TSIMM-er
33. toilet	klo	kloh
34. I	ich	eekh
35. you	du	doo
36. love	liebe	LEE-beh
37. sleep	schlaf	shloff
38. train	zug	tsoog
39. The bill, please	die Rechnung, bitte	dee RECK-nung, BIT-teh
40. friend	freund	froint
41. water	wasser	VOSS-ehr
42. castle	schloss	shlohss
43. How are you/ I'm fine, thanks	wie geht es?/ Es geht mir gut, dahnke	vee GATES/ ess GATE mehr GOOT, DONG-kuh
44. Tourist Information	Reiseburo	RIE-suh-BYOO-ro

Foreign Phrases

ITALIAN

1.	hello	bongiorno	bohn-ZHOOR-no
2.	goodbye	ciao	chow
3.	see you later	civediamo	chee vey-dee-OMM-o
4.	goodnight	buona notte	BWONN-ah NOT-tay
5.	please	per favore	pair fah-VOR-ay
6.	thank you	grazie	GRAH-tsee-ay
7.	yes/no	si/no	see/no
8.	one/two/three	uno/due/tray	oo-noh/doo-ay/tray
9.	cheap/expensive	economico/caro	ay-koh-NO-mee-koh/CARR-o
10.	good/bad	buone/cattivo	BWON-o/kaht-TEE-vo
11.	beautiful/ugly	bello/brutto	BEHL-lo/BROOT-to
12.	big/small	grande/piccolo	GRAHN-day/PEEKkoh-lo
13.	fast/slow	rapido/lento	RAHH-pee-do/LEHN-to
14.	very	molto	MOHL-to
15.	where is . . . ?	dov'e . . . ?	do-VAY
16.	how much . . . ?	quanto?	KWAHN-to
17.	I don't understand	Non capisco	nohn kay-PEESS-ko
18.	what do you call this?	che cosi questo?	kay KO-see KWAY-sto
19.	I'm lost	mi sono perso	mee SOH-no PEHR-so
20.	I'm tired	sono stanco	SOH-no STAHNG-ko
21.	I'm hungry	ho fame	oh FAH-may
22.	food	cibo	CHEE-bo
23.	grocery store	drogheria	dro-GAY-ree-ah
24.	picnic	picnic	picnic
25.	delicious	delizioso	day-leet-see-OH-so
26.	market	mercato	mayr-COT-to
27.	drunk	ubriaco	oo-bree-AH-co
28.	money	denaro	day-NAHR-ro
29.	station	stazione	STAHT-see-OH-nay
30.	private accommodations	camera	CAH-may-rah
31.	toilet	toilet	toy-LET
32.	I	io	ee-OH
33.	you	lei	lay
34.	love	amore	ah-MOH-ray
35.	sleep	dormire	dor-MEER-ay
36.	train	treno	TREN-no
37.	The bill, please	Il conto, prego	ell KON-to, pray-go
38.	friend	amico	ah-mee-ko
39.	water/tap water	acqua/acqua naturale	AH-kwa nah-toor-ALL—ay
40.	castle	castello	kah-STELL-o
41.	church	chiesa	kee-AY-za
42.	How are you?	come va?	KO-may VAH
43.	Tourist Information	ufficio informazioni	oo-FEE-see-o EEN-for-MOTZ-ee-OH-nee
44.	You're welcome	prego	PRAY-go
45.	Doing sweet nothing	dolce far niente	DOL-chay far nee-YEN-tay

FRENCH

1. hello	bonjour	bohn-ZHOOR
2. goodbye	au revoir	oh-VWAH
3. see you later	a bientot	ah byuhn-TOH
4. goodnight	bonne nuit	bohn NWEE
5. please	s'il vous plait	see voo PLAY
6. thank you	merci	mehr-SEE
7. yes/no	oui/non	wee/noh
8. one/two/three	un/deux/trois	uh/DOO/twah
9. cheap/expensive	bon marche/cher	bohn mar-shay/shehr
10. good/bad	bon/mauvais	bohn/mo-VAY
11. beautiful/ugly	joli/laid	zho-LEE/lay
12. big/small	grand/petit	grahn/pehTEE
13. fast/slow	rapide/lent	rah-PEED/lehn
14. very	tres	tray
15. where is . . . ?	ou est . . . ?	oo ay
16. how much . . . ?	combien	kohm-bee-UHN
17. I don't understand	je ne comprends pas	zhuh neh KOHM-prahn PAH
18. What do you call this?	qu'est-ce que c'est?	KESS koo SAY
19. I'm lost	je me suis perdu	zhuh meh swee pehr-DOO
20. complete price (everything included)	tout est compris	too-tay kohm-PREE
21. Im tired	je suis fatigue	zhuh swee fah-tee-GAY
22. I'm hungry	j'ai faim	zhay fam
23. cheers!	sante!	sahn-TAY
24. food	nourriture	new-ree-TOOR
25. grocery store	epicerie	eh-PEES-eh-REE
26. picnic	pique-nique	peek-neek
27. delicious	delicieux	de-lee-syoh
28. market	marche	mar-SHAY
29. drunk	soul	SOO
30. money	argent	ar-ZHA
31. station	gare	gar
32. private accommodations	chambre	shambr
33. toilet	w.c.	VAY say
34. I	je	zhuh
35. you	vous	voo
36. love	amour	ah-MOOR
37. sleep	sommeil	so-MAY
38. train	train	tran
39. The bill, please	L'addition, s'il vous plait	lah-dee-see-OHN, see voo play
40. friend	ami	ah-MEE
41. water/tap water	eau/eau douce	OH/OL dooss
42. castle	chateau	shat-TOH
43. How are you?/I'm fine	ca va?/ca va	sah VAH
44. Tourist Information	syndicat d'initiative	san-dee-KAH dan-EE-see-ah-TEEV

Train Schedules

These are the train time tables for this proposed European tour. *Use these for planning only* to give you an idea of how many trains leave a day and how long the trips take. These times will change a lot by the time you get this book. We cut out all the exceptions and "fine print" so don't use these for navigating. Confirm your departure plans upon arrival at the train station's information desk.

If you can't find your train trip listed, look for it in reverse order (from your destination to where you are) and assume the rides will be as common and as fast or slow.

Key

☒	Change trains	⌐	Sleeping car.
ℝ	Seat reservation compulsory	⊢	Couchette car.
x	Weekdays, except public holidays	✕	Dining car or buffet car

Amsterdam to ...

Paris Nord

7 00	12 52
7 48	13 52
8 53	14 10 TEE ✕
10 53	16 55
12 26	18 55 ☒ Bruxelles Nord IC
13 26	19 44 ☒ Bruxelles Midi TEE ✕
14 26	20 34 ☒ Bruxelles Midi IC ✕
15 52	22 06 x
17 53	23 10 TEE ✕
20 26	6 42 ⊢

London Victoria ☽

6 47?	14 48	☒ Roosendaal
		☒ Oostende ⇒ ☒ Dover
8 56	16 48	☒ Roosendaal
		☒ Oostende ⇒ ☒ Dover
9 30	19 23?	☒ Hoek van Holland ⌐
		☒ Harwich
11 56	19 32	☒ Roosendaal
		☒ Oostende ⇒ ☒ Dover
14 56	22 32	☒ Roosendaal
		☒ Oostende ⇒ ☒ Dover
21 16	9 14?	☒ Hoek van Holland ⌐
		☒ Harwich

København

Ⓦ 8 01	19 45	☒ Hamburg Hbf IC ✕
Ⓢ 8 01	19 29	
Ⓦ 19 42	9 09	☒ Amersfoort ⊢
Ⓢ 20 01	8 09	⊢

Koblenz

6 57	10 55	IC ✕
7 49	11 40	TEE ✕
8 38	13 07	✕
8 53	13 33	via Nijmegen
10 17	14 49	☒ Köln IC ✕
12 17	16 49	☒ Köln IC ✕
14 25	18 25	IC ✕
14 53	19 45	
17 19	21 43	
19 19	0 31	via Nijmegen
19 49	0 50	

Frankfurt to ...

Amsterdam CS

7 09	12 26	IC ✕
7 24	13 15	
9 29	15 42	IC ✕ ☒ Köln
10 29	16 43	IC ✕ ☒ Köln
11 29	17 44	IC ✕ ☒ Köln
12 29	18 42	IC ✕ ☒ Köln
14 29	20 03	IC ✕ ☒ Köln TEE ✕
15 29	20 52	IC ✕
16 29	22 26	IC ✕ ☒ Köln
18 11	0 19	☒ Köln

München

4 41	6 57	
7 40	10 05	
8 55	11 03	IC ✕
11 20	13 50	
12 08	13 54	TEE ✕
12 25	14 33	IC ✕
14 12	16 25	
15 00	17 19	
18 38	21 01	
19 12	21 26	
20 00	22 10	✕

Berlin Zool. Garten

8 53	16 17	✕
9 23	17 06	IC ✕ ☒ Hannover ✕
10 25	18 17	IC ✕ ☒ Hannover ✕
13 23	20 40	IC ✕ ☒ Hannover ✕
15 26	22 36	
22 35	6 13	⌐ ⊢

København

0 06	12 09	⌐ ⊢ ☒ Hamburg
0 30	14 09	⌐ ⊢ ☒ Hamburg
Ⓢ 8 23	19 29	IC ✕ ☒ Hamburg IC ✕
9 23	19 45	IC ✕ ☒ Hamburg IC ✕
12 23	22 50	IC ✕ ☒ Hamburg
16 31	6 45	⌐ ⊢

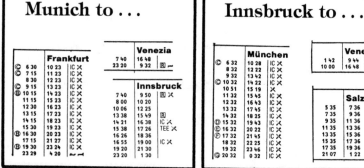

Munich to ...

Frankfurt

Ⓒ 6 30	10 23	IC ✕
Ⓒ 7 15	11 23	IC ✕
8 30	12 23	IC ✕
Ⓒ 9 15	13 23	IC ✕
Ⓑ 10 15	14 23	IC ✕
11 15	15 23	IC ✕
12 30	16 23	IC ✕
13 15	17 23	IC ✕
14 15	18 23	IC ✕
15 30	19 23	IC ✕
Ⓑ 16 30	20 23	IC ✕
17 15	21 27	IC ✕
Ⓑ 19 30	23 23	IC ✕
23 29	4 20	⌐ ⊢

Venezia

7 40	16 48	
23 20	9 32	ℝ ⊢

Innsbruck

7 40	9 50	ℝ ✕
8 00	10 20	
10 06	12 25	
13 38	15 49	ℝ
14 21	16 38	IC ✕
15 38	17 26	TEE ✕
16 26	18 36	
16 55	19 00	IC ✕
19 20	21 30	
23 20	1 30	

Innsbruck to ...

München

Ⓒ 6 32	10 28	IC ✕
8 32	12 22	IC ✕
9 32	13 42	IC ✕
Ⓒ 10 32	14 22	IC ✕
10 51	15 19	✕
11 32	15 45	IC ✕
12 32	16 43	IC ✕
13 32	17 45	IC ✕
14 32	18 25	IC ✕
Ⓢ 15 32	19 43	IC ✕
Ⓔ 16 32	20 22	IC ✕
Ⓕ 17 32	21 45	IC ✕
18 32	22 25	IC ✕
19 32	23 46	IC ✕
Ⓖ 20 32	0 32	IC ✕

Venezia

1 42	9 44	⊢
10 00	16 48	✕

Salzburg

5 35	7 36	
7 35	9 36	
9 35	11 36	✕
11 35	13 36	✕
13 35	15 36	✕
15 35	17 36	✕
17 35	19 36	✕
21 07	1 22	

Salzburg to . . .

	München				
4 00	5 54	13 45	15 33		
5 12	7 03	14 47	16 58		
6 12	8 19	15 32	17 28	✕	
6 55	8 29	16 13	18 24		
7 55	9 41	18 39	20 22	✕	
8 22	10 10	18 52	20 35	✕	
8 47	10 52	19 05	20 46		
10 12	12 18	19 54	21 45		
10 42	12 34	✕	20 47	22 42	✕
11 56	13 34	✕	21 32	23 30	
12 26	14 02	IC ✕	21 45	23 35	✕

Venice to . . .

	Roma Termini			Firenze	
			0 38	4 44	⇌ ⊶
0 38	8 35	⇌ ⊶	5 25	9 24	✕
5 25	12 55	✕	8 04	11 05	ℝ
8 04	14 05	ℝ ☒ Firenze TEE ℝ	10 22	14 43	✕
10 22	18 50	✕	11 00	14 14	ℝ ✕
11 00	17 10	ℝ ✕	11 42	15 41	
11 42	19 48	✕	15 44	19 36	
15 35	23 09	✕	16 25	20 32	✕
22 48	7 15	⇌ ⊶	20 55	0 47	

Florence to . . .

	Venezia SL		Pisa		Pisa			Roma Termini	
			5 55	6 48			4 54	8 35	
			7 00	7 54	14 23	15 32	6 55	9 40	Rapido
6 23	10 37	✕	7 25	8 23	16 20	17 14	8 02	12 05	
9 50	13 28	✕	8 36	10 00	17 32	18 29	9 34	12 55	✕
10 52	14 36	✕	9 40	10 36	18 22	19 40	10 37	13 45	✕
13 27	16 37	ℝ ✕	11 16	12 30	19 02	19 57	11 40	14 50	⟨
15 00	18 54	✕	12 00	13 10	20 43	22 10	14 22	17 10	ℝ ✕
16 28	20 20	✕	13 20	14 30	21 54	23 23	14 50	18 50	✕
20 20	0 04	✕			23 00	0 01	15 51	19 48	✕
							16 17	19 13	Rapido ✕
							16 43	20 07	✕
							17 50	21 12	✕
							18 50	22 50	✕
							20 12	23 00	TEE ℝ ✕
							20 42	23 50	✕

Rome to . . .

	Firenze			Genova				
			0 41	7 15	⇌ ⊶			
			7 20	13 01	ℝ ✕			
6 45	9 40	✕	8 30	15 55				
7 50	10 36	TEE ℝ ✕	10 55	17 35	✕			
8 00	11 17	✕	12 10	18 05	✕			
9 35	13 17	✕	14 00	19 47	ℝ ✕			
10 38	14 50	✕	15 30	21 18	✕			
11 30	14 13	TEE ℝ ✕	16 30	22 05				
12 23	16 18	✕	16 50	23 40				
13 45	16 45	Rapido ✕	18 48	23 45	ℝ ✕			
14 35	18 08	✕	23 05	5 41	⇌ ⊶			
16 05	19 10	✕						
18 05	22 09	✕	7 50	**Paris Lyon**				
19 28	22 51			23 00	TEE ℝ ✕ ☒ Milano			
20 24	23 51		15 30	8 57	TEE ℝ ✕			
21 45	0 38		18 48	10 06	⇌ ⊶ ✕			

Genoa to . . .

	Nice			Roma Termini			Firenze	
5 58	10 02		0 20	7 08	⇌ ⊶			
8 23	11 16		1 20	8 44	⇌ ⊶			
8 45	13 39		5 45	10 44	ℝ			
15 30	19 18		8 14	13 55	✕			
17 45	22 02		8 45	16 48		8 14	12 18	☒ Pisa
18 40	23 36		10 09	15 30	ℝ ✕	10 09	13 48	ℝ ✕ ☒ Pisa
			11 47	18 37	✕	11 47	16 20	✕ ☒ Pisa
			12 50	19 55	✕	12 55	17 40	✕ ☒ Pisa
			15 59	22 15		13 50	18 00	☒ Pisa
			18 32	23 55	ℝ ✕	15 59	20 05	✕ ☒ Pisa
			22 35	4 21⁾	⇌ ⊶	18 32	21 46	ℝ ✕ ☒ Pisa
			23 32	5 27⁾	⇌ ⊶	19 38	23 30	☒ Pisa
			23 46	5 48⁾	⇌ ⊶			

Bern to . . .

	Genova				Roma Termini		
	29 V 83–14 I 84				**29 V 83–14 I 84**		
7 21	13 35			6 21	17 45	☒ Milano TEE ℝ ✕	
8 13	14 53	IC ☒ Milano ✕		8 13	19 13	IC ☒ Milano Rapido ✕	
9 21	16 00	☒ Milano		11 21	23 00	☒ Milano TEE ℝ ✕	
11 21	18 20	☒ Milano		17 21	6 30⁾	☒ Milano ⇌ ⊶	
12 54	20 07	☒ Milano		19 21	8 15	⇌ ⊶⁾	
17 13	23 18	☒ Brig TEE ℝ			**15 I–2 VI 84**		
		☒ Milano ℝ ✕		6 21	17 45	☒ Milano TEE ℝ ✕	
17 21	0 29	☒ Milano		8 13	19 13	IC ☒ Milano Rapido ✕	
29 V–22 X				9 21	23 00	☒ Milano	
	15 I–2 VI 84			16 13	6 30⁾	☒ Milano ⇌ ⊶	
8 13	14 53			19 21	8 15	⇌ ⊶⁾	
9 21	16 00	☒ Milano		¹⁾ Roma Tiburtina			
13 21	20 07	☒ Milano		²⁾ from/de/ab Brig			
16 13	22 02	IC ☒ Brig ☒ Milano					

	Milano Centrale	
	29 V 83–14 I 84	
6 21	11 00	
8 13	12 25	IC
9 21	13 55	
11 21	16 00	
12 54	17 00	
14 21	19 05	☒ Brig IC
17 13	21 00	☒ Brig TEE ℝ
17 21	22 00	
19 21	24 00	

	Strasbourg		
6 45	9 45	IC ☒ Basel ✕	
11 23	14 37	☒ Olten ☒ Basel IC ✕	
13 45	17 06	☒ Basel	
14 45	17 51	✕¹⁾	
17 45	21 40	☒ Basel	
21 45	2 08	☒ Basel	

	Paris Lyon		
	29 V 83–14 I 84		
6 53	12 59¹⁾	☒ Belfort IC ✕	
7 20	13 35	✕²⁾	
13 47	19 50		
17 16	23 25	IC ✕ ☒ Lausanne	
		TEE ℝ ✕	
23 02	6 23	⊶	
¹⁾ Paris Est			
²⁾ Frasne–Paris			
	15 I–2 VI 84		
6 37	11 26	☒ Frasne TGV ✕	
11 16	16 23	✕ ☒ Lausanne TGV ✕	
16 40	21 31	☒ Frasne TGV ✕	
18 16	23 26	✕ ☒ Lausanne TGV ✕	
23 02	6 23	⊶	

Sample Train Schedules

Paris to . . .

dp/ab Paris Nord

London Victoria ⏰

ⓒ 6 52	11 40¹⁾	☒ Boulogne ⛴ ☒ Dover
ⓓ 6 52	11 40¹⁾	☒ Calais ⛴ ☒ Dover
ⓔ 8 10	14 48	☒ Boulogne ⛴ ☒ Folkestone
ⓔ 9 20	13 40¹⁾	☒ Boulogne ⛴ ☒ Dover
ⓕ 10 37	16 55	☒ Boulogne ⛴
		☒ Folkestone
ⓔ 10 45²⁾	18 46	☒ Dieppe ⛴ ☒ Newhaven
ⓕ 11 25	15 40¹⁾	☒ Boulogne ⛴ ☒ Dover
ⓖ 12 17	16 43¹⁾	☒ Boulogne ⛴ ☒ Dover
ⓔ 12 20	19 02	☒ Calais ⛴ ☒ Folkestone
ⓕ 13 00	17 43¹⁾	☒ Boulogne ⛴ ☒ Dover
ⓔ 14 20	19 40¹⁾	☒ Boulogne ⛴ ☒ Dover
ⓔ 22 35	8 10	☒ Dunkerque ⛴ ☒ Dover
ⓗ 22 36²⁾	6 57	☒ Dieppe ⛴ ☒ Newhaven

Amsterdam CS

7 19	12 30	TEE ✕
7 48	14 13	
10 23	16 32	✕
11 37	17 05	TEE ✕ ☒ Bruxelles Midi
12 56	19 05	IC ☒ Bruxelles Midi
15 18	21 33	
16 45	22 38	IC
17 41	22 45	TEE ✕
18 40	0 05	TEE ✕ ☒ Bruxelles Midi
23 15	9 43	⊸

dp/ab Paris Austerlitz

Madrid-Chamartin

✕ 6 45	21 52	✕ ☒ Irun IC ✕
14 00	8 34	✕ ☒ Irun ⊸
17 50	10 05	⊸¹⁾ ☒ Hendaye IC
20 00	8 55	only/seulement/nur ⊸ ✕
21 55	17 48	⊸¹⁾ ☒ Irun ✕
22 50	16 21	only/seulement/nur ⊸ ⊸
		☒ Irun IC ✕

Colmar to . . .

Paris Est	
0 08	6 08 ⊸
5 26	9 37 ✕
7 45	11 36 IC ✕
8 16	12 39 ✕
10 20	14 18 IC ✕
12 51	17 20 ✕
15 49	20 11 ✕
17 16	22 05 ✕
19 17	23 11 IC ✕

Brussels to . . .

London Victoria ⏰

6 00	13 06	☒ Oostende ⛴ ☒ Dover
7 00	11 17	☒ Oostende 🚢 ☒ Dover
8 13	15 10	☒ Oostende ⛴ ☒ Dover
10 00	14 33	☒ Oostende 🚢 ☒ Dover
11 55	16 36	☒ Oostende ⛴ ☒ Dover
11 55	18 48	☒ Oostende ⛴ ☒ Dover
15 00	19 17	☒ Oostende 🚢 ☒ Dover
18 00	22 17	☒ Oostende 🚢 ☒ Dover
23 06	7 15	☒ Oostende ⛴ ☒ Folkestone
23 41	7 15	☒ Oostende ⛴ ☒ Folkestone

Amsterdam

6 18	9 43			
7 09	10 06			
8 09¹⁾	11 05		Paris Nord	
9 09	12 05			
10 09	13 05	0 32	6 42	⊸
11 06	14 23	7 30	10 05	TEE ✕
12 09	15 05	8 15	11 18	
13 09	16 05	10 06	12 52	
14 09	17 05	11 03	13 52	✕
15 09	18 05	11 43	14 10	TEE ✕
16 09	19 05	14 07	16 55	
17 02	20 05	16 08	18 55	IC
18 09	21 05	17 17	19 44	TEE ✕
19 09	22 05	17 53	20 34	IC ✕
20 09	23 06	19 15	22 06	✕
21 11	0 05	20 42	23 11	TEE ✕

Madrid to . . .

dp/ab Madrid-Chamartin

Paris Austerlitz

8 00	23 21	☒ Hendaye ✕
12 35	7 45	✕ ☒ Hendaye
18 08	10 33	⊸ ✕
19 40	8 48	Ⓝ ⊸ ✕
22 05	16 19	⊸ ⊸ ☒ Hendaye ✕

Tours to . . .

Paris Austerlitz

6 34	8 45	
7 12	9 27	
7 53	10 00	☒ St-Pierre-des-Corps ✕
8 58	11 27	
9 33	11 33	☒ St-Pierre-des-Corps ✕
10 27	13 03	
11 49	13 33	☒ St-Pierre-des-Corps ✕
13 13	15 33	
14 17	16 19	☒ St-Pierre-des-Corps ✕
15 37	18 13	
16 30	18 46	☒ St-Pierre-des-Corps ✕
16 51	19 00	☒ St-Pierre-des-Corps ✕
17 19	19 24	
18 15	20 30	
19 38	21 38	☒ St-Pierre-des-Corps
20 56	23 12	☒ St-Pierre-des-Corps
21 34	23 21	☒ St-Pierre-des-Corps

London to . . .

dp/ab London Victoria

Amsterdam CS

8 44	17 35	☒ Dover 🚢 ☒ Oostende
		☒ Roosendaal
9 20¹⁾	20 55	☒ Harwich ⛴
		☒ Hoek van Holland
9 30	21 05	☒ Dover ⛴ ☒ Oostende
		☒ Gent ☒ Antwerpen
11 30	20 35	☒ Dover 🚢 ☒ Oostende
		☒ Roosendaal
13 44	22 35	☒ Dover 🚢 ☒ Oostende
		☒ Roosendaal
19 40¹⁾	9 01	☒ Harwich ⛴
		☒ Hoek van Holland
21 44	9 43	☒ Folkestone ⛴
		☒ Oostende ☒ Antwerpen

dp/ab London Victoria

Paris Nord

7 48¹⁾	14 15	☒ Dover ⛴ ☒ Boulogne
7 50	18 10²⁾	☒ Newhaven ⛴ ☒ Dieppe
ⓒ 8 00	16 15	☒ Folkestone ⛴ ☒ Boulogne
10 00¹⁾	16 32	☒ Dover ⛴ ☒ Boulogne
10 30	18 20	☒ Dover ⛴ ☒ Calais
12 00¹⁾	18 25	☒ Dover ⛴ ☒ Boulogne
13 58	22 30	☒ Folkestone ⛴ ☒ Calais ✕
14 00¹⁾	20 40	☒ Dover ⛴ ☒ Boulogne
ⓓ 16 00¹⁾	23 02	☒ Dover ⛴ ☒ Boulogne
ⓔ 20 10	6 25²⁾	☒ Newhaven ⛴ ☒ Dieppe
20 58	8 43	☒ Dover ⛴ ☒ Dunkerque

dp/ab London Victoria

Oostende

8 44	13 15	☒ Dover 🚢
9 30	16 15	☒ Dover ⛴
11 30	16 00	☒ Dover 🚢
13 30	20 05	☒ Dover 🚢
13 44	18 20	☒ Dover 🚢
15 58	20 30	☒ Dover 🚢
18 58	23 35	☒ Dover 🚢
21 44	5 10	☒ Folkestone ⛴

dp/ab London King's Cross

Edinburgh

ⓒ 0 05	9 00	⊸
ⓒ 8 00	12 47	✕¹⁾
ⓒ 9 00	13 46	✕¹⁾
ⓖ 9 30	15 18	
ⓒ 10 00	14 30	✕¹⁾
ⓖ 10 00	15 37	
	10 35	15 34 ✕¹⁾
ⓒ 11 00	15 41 ✕¹⁾
ⓖ 11 00	16 41	
ⓒ 12 00	16 47 ✕¹⁾
ⓖ 12 00	17 30	
ⓒ 13 00	17 46 ✕¹⁾
ⓖ 13 00	18 25	
ⓒ 14 00	18 48 ✕¹⁾
ⓖ 14 00	19 27	
ⓒ 15 00	19 52 ✕¹⁾
ⓖ 15 00	20 11	
	16 00	20 45 ✕¹⁾
	17 00	21 45 ✕¹⁾
	18 00	22 52 ✕¹⁾
ⓑ 23 20	7 05	only/seulement/nur ⊸
ⓑ 23 50	8 35	only/seulement/nur ⊸
ⓒ①–⑥		
¹⁾ ①–⑥		

Here are the schedules for the bus ride through the best of medieval Germany (about Frankfurt to Munich) and the boat ride past the best castles on the Rhine (Koblenze to Bingen). Both rides are included free with the Eurailpass. These connect at Weisbaden and give you the most interesting way to sightsee your way from Holland to Munich and Bavaria.

Romantic Road Bus Tour

Table 1635 WIESBADEN – MÜNCHEN
DB/DTG Line 190
Daily, March 19–Nov. 7.

0700	dep.	Wiesbaden (Nassauer Hof) .... arr.	2045	...
0705	dep.	Wiesbaden (Hbf.) .... arr.	2040	...
0815	dep.	Frankfurt/Main (Hbf.) .... arr.	1955	...
1000	arr.	Würzburg (Hbf.) .... dep.	1810	... †
1015	dep.		arr.	1809	...
1135	arr.	Rothenburg/Tauber .... dep.	1700	...
1345	dep.	(Schrannenplatz) ✗ .... arr.	1515	
1430	dep.	Feuchtwangen (Markt) .... dep.	1430	
1445	arr.	Dinkelsbühl ✗ .... dep.	1415	
1530	dep.	(Schweinemarkt) .... arr.	1235	
1605	dep.	Nördlingen (Verkehrsbüro) .... dep.	1155	...
1635	dep.	Donauwörth (Kirche) .... dep.	1105	...
1735	arr.	Augsburg (Hbf.) .... dep.	1015	...
1745	dep.		arr.	1010	...
1855	arr.	München Hbf., (Starnberger Bahnhof) .... dep.	0900	...

†—Does not take up or set down at Würzburg June 11–Sept. 30. Connects at Rothenburg with Table 1636.

Table 1636 WÜRZBURG – FÜSSEN
DB/DTG Line 190
Daily, June 11–Sept. 18.

0900	dep.	Würzburg (Hbf.) .... arr.	1920	...
1005	dep.	Bad Mergentheim (Hbf.) .... dep.	1815	...
1200	arr.	Rothenburg/Tauber .... dep.	1700	...
1310	dep.	(Schrannenplatz) ✗ .... arr.	1545	...
1355	dep.	Feuchtwangen (Markt) .... dep.	1505	...
1410	arr.	Dinkelsbühl .... dep.	1445	...
1445	dep.	(Schweinemarkt) .... arr.	1315	...
1520	dep.	Nördlingen (Verkehrsamt) .... dep.	1245	...
1555	dep.	Donauwörth (Kirche) .... dep.	1215	...
1645	arr.	Augsburg (Hbf.) .... dep.	1130	...
1715	dep.		arr.	1100	...
1815	dep.	Landsberg (Hbf.) .... dep.	1010	...
1955	arr.	Füssen (Postamt) .... dep.	0815	...

Connection Mannheim–Rothenburg by Line 189:

0715	dep.	Mannheim (Hbf.) .... arr.	2045	...
0745	dep.	Heidelberg (Hbf.) .... dep.	2025	...
0825	dep.	Eberbach .... dep.	1952	...
0912	dep.	Bad Friedrichshall .... dep.	1909	...
1200	arr.	Rothenburg/Tauber .... dep.	1650	...

Rhine Cruise

Table 700 KÖLN-DÜSSELDORFER DEUTSCHE RHEINSCHIFFAHRT AG
KD GERMAN RHINE LINE

Tar. km	⚓		S	D	Exp O	H	N	R	E	H	P	fast C‡	A	G	J		C	F	Q	H		M
100	Koblenz {	arr.			1100			1120		1335 1355								1545	1750	..		1900
		dep.	9 00		1105 1030		1130 1130 1340	1400 1400	1400			1430									1905
105	Niederlahnstein ....dep.		9 24		1055		1155 1155					1425	1455									1930
112	Brauhach ....dep.		9 58		1130		1225 1225		1445 1445	1455		1525									2005
121	Boppard ....dep.	9 05 1040		1130 1220		1250 1315 1315	d	1525 1525 1544		1615									2045
137	St. Goarshausen ....dep.	1015 1150			1335 1330 1400	1425 1440		1625 1625 1655		1725									
137	St. Goar ....dep.	1025 1155			1150 1340 1340	1435 1435 1445		1630 1630 1700		1735									
154	Bacharach ....dep.	1130 1255			1208 1440 1445	1505 1540 1545		1725 1725 1803		1840									
166	Assmannshausen ....dep.	1235 1350			1535 1535	1600 1635 1640		1810 1810 1905		1935									
170	Bingen ....dep.	1305 1420			1228 1605 1602	1630 1705 1710		1835 1835 1930		2000									
172	Rüdesheim ....arr.	1320 1430			1233 1615 1620	1640 1715 1720		1850 1850 1940		2010									
187	Eltville ....dep.				1720		1745 1820 1825		1955 1955										
195	Wiesbaden-Biebrich ...arr.				1300 1805 1800	1835 1910 1910		2040 2040										
200	Mainz ....arr.				1310 1825 1820	1855 1930 1930		2100 2100										
225	Frankfurt/Main ....arr.					2130													

Tar. km	⚓		A	fast L‡	L	BB	J		F		B	N	T	Q	E		S		P		Exp O
25	Frankfurt/Main ....dep.									7 15											
0	Mainz ....dep.		8 45 8 45							1015 1000		1045								1425
5	Wiesbaden-Biebrich ...dep.		8 05 9 05							1035 1020		1045								1433
13	Eltville ....dep.		9 25 9 25							1040		1125								
28	Rüdesheim ....dep.		1015 1015 9 50 9 50						1145 1130		1240		1400					1500
30	Bingen ....dep.		1030 1030 1015 1015						1200 1145		1235		1415					1505
34	Assmannshausen ....dep.		1045 1045 1030 1030						1215 1200		1250		1430					
46	Bacharach ....dep.		1110 1110 1108 1108						1240 1235		1325		1505					
63	St. Goar ....dep.		1140 1140						1310 1320		1410		1550					
63	St. Goarshausen ....dep.		1145 1145 1200 1200						1315 1325		1420		1600			d	1540
79	Boppard ....dep.		1225 1225 1240 1240								1510		1645					1555
88	Brauhach ....dep.		1250		1310						1540		1715					
95	Niederlahnstein ....dep.				1332						1602		1737					
100	Koblenz {	arr.	1330 1320 1350								1620		1755		1720 1618			
		dep.		1330							1550 1625		1800		1725 1620			

A— Daily, Apr. 20–30.
B— Suns., May 1–June 2.
C— Daily, May 1–Sept. 18.
D— Daily, April 20–Oct. 30.
E— Daily, June 12–Sept. 18.
F— April 21, 22 and daily April 25–Sept. 18.
G— Daily, Sept. 19–Oct. 30.
H— Daily, Sept. 19–Oct. 2.
J— Daily, Oct. 3–30.
K— Daily, April 20–Oct. 2.
L— Daily, May 1–Oct. 2.
M— Daily, June 12–Sept. 18 (not Koblenz-Boppard on Sats.).
N— Daily except Weds. May 1–Sept. 18.
O— Express service, daily except Mons., May 1–Oct. 2 by hydrofoil Rheinpfeil. Also runs Apr. 21, 22, 28, 29, Oct. 8, 9, 15, 16, 22, 23, 29, 30. Special fares apply.
P— Mons., Tues. and Thurs., July 11–Aug. 18 also June 13, 20, 27, July 4, Aug. 22, 29, Sept. 5, 12.

Q—Daily Sept. 19–Oct. 2, also Sats. and Suns. July 10–Aug
R— Daily, Oct. 3–9.
S— Daily, June 12–Sept. 18, except Aug. 27, Sept. 3, 10, 1;
T— Daily, Sept. 19–Oct. 9.
W— Daily, May 8–Oct. 16.
Y— Daily, May 8–Sept. 11.
Z— Daily, Sept. 12–Oct. 15.
AA—Daily, Sept. 12–Oct. 16.
BB—Daily, Oct. 3–30.
b— Daily except Mons., July 10–Aug. 21.
d— Rhine/Moselle excursion to/from Kobern (Moselle).
‡— Fast ship, supplement payable (not applicable between and Köln Sept. 19–Oct. 2).
§— Fast ship, supplement payable applicable only from to Mainz.

SAMPLE EUROPEAN TRAIN TRIPS

How long they take and how much they cost in 1985.

From .... To		2nd Class (One Way)	Journey Time (Hours)
Amsterdam	Brussels	$19	3½
	Frankfurt	42	6
	Koben	72	12
	Munich	74	12
	Paris	42	5½
	Vienna	96	15
	Zurich	78	11
Athens	Munich	94	39
	Beograd	43	20
Barcelona	Marseilles	38	8
	Madrid	38	8
	Rome	81	20
	Paris	79	12
Berlin	Hamburg	22	3½
	Brussels	64	10
	Warsaw	32	9
	Paris	85	14
Brindisi	Rome	25	7
	Patras	75	17
Kopenhavn	Koln	69	11
	Oslo	53	10
	Rome	155	31
	Paris	107	14
	Stockholm	44	8
Madrid	Lisbon	30	9
	Sevilla	30	6
	Paris	93	16
Oslo	Trondheim	50	8
	Stavanger	52	9
	Bergen	45	7
Paris	Marseilles	63	8
	Rome	80	17
	Venice	71	13
	Vienna	104	15
	Zurich	49	7½
Rome	Venice	22	6

1st Class tickets cost 50% more than 2nd Class.

There are faster and slower trains — these times are average.

Any journey of 6 hours or longer can be taken overnight.

From this list you should be able to estimate the time and money required for any European train journey. Remember times and costs of journeys per inch on the map are roughly similar at equal latitudes. So to estimate time and cost of a southern journey, compare it to a southern entry on this list. Northern trains are faster and more expensive. Don't worry about more exact information until you get to Europe. Plan with this chart, cocky confidence and a spirit of adventure.

──BACK DOOR CATALOG──

ALL ITEMS FIELD TESTED, HIGHLY RECOMMENDED, COMPETELY
GUARANTEED AND DISCOUNTED BELOW RETAIL.

Back door Combination Ruck Sack / Suitcase $60

At 9'' x 21'' x 13'', this specially designed, sturdy functional bag is maximum carry-on-the-plane size. (Fits under the seat.) Constructed of rugged waterproof nylon Cordura material, with hide-away shoulder-straps, waist belt, and – for toting as a suitcase – top and side handles and a detachable shoulder strap. Perimeter zippers allow easy access to the roomy (2200 cu. in.) central compartment. Two small outside pockets are perfect for maps and other frequently used items. Nine hundred travellers took these bags around the world last year and returned satisfied. Comparable bags cost much more. If you're looking for maximum "carry-on size" and a suitcase that can be converted into a back pack, this is your best bet. Available in navy blue, black, or gray.

Money belt $6.00

Required! Ultra-light, sturdy, under-the-pants, nylon pouch just big enough to carry the essentials comfortably. I'll never travel without one and I hope you won't either. Beige, nylon zipper, one size fits all, with instructions.

Sturdy Day Rucksack $8.00

This blue nylon bag is ideal for day-tripping. Leave your suitcase in the hotel, on the bus, or at the station and run around with this on your back. Folds into its own pocket. Very light and sturdy.

Eurail Passes
Send Eurail form with check for the pass and a proposed itinerary and list of questions. Receive within two weeks train pass and free cassette tape-recorded evaluation of trip plans by registered mail. Because of this unique service, Rick Steves sells more train passes than anyone in the Pacific Northwest.

RICK STEVES BUDGET TRAVEL SEMINARS are taught to groups and colleges throughout the West Coast. Write for info.

All orders include postage, rubber universal sink stopper and a one year's subscription to our quarterly Back Door Travel Newsletter. Send checks to:

"EUROPE THROUGH THE BACK DOOR,"

111 4th Ave. N.   Edmonds, WA 98020   tel. (206) 771-8303

Other European Travel Guides
by Rick Steves You're Sure to Enjoy!

Europe 101: History, Art and Culture for the Traveler
376 pages, $9.95
Finally, travelers have Europe 101! The first and only travelers guide to Europe's history and art. Full of boiled down, practical information to make your sightseeing more meaningful and enjoyable. Your "passport to culture" in a fun, easy to read manual.

Europe Through the Back Door
1985 Edition, Revised and Expanded, 376 pages, $9.95
The lessons of 14 years of budget European travel packaged into 376 fun to read pages. All the basic skills of budget independent travel, plus 34 special "Back Doors" where you'll find the Europe most tourists miss. Sure to make you a seasoned traveler on your first trip.

COMING SOON!   **Great Britain in 22 Days**
               Spain & Portugal in 22 Days

I'd like to order the terrific travel guides checked below. . .

Quantity	Title	Each	Total
	Europe Through the Back Door — *Steves*	$9.95	
	Europe 101: History, Art & Culture for Travelers — *Steves*	$9.95	
	Europe in 22 Days — *Steves*	$4.95	
	Complete Guide to Bed & Breakfasts, Inns & Guesthouses In the U.S. & Canada — *Lanier*	$10.95	
	The People's Guide to Mexico (Revised) — *Franz*	$10.95	
	The People's Guide to Camping in Mexico — *Franz*	$10.00	
	The On & Off the Road Cookbook — *Franz & Havens*	$8.50	

Send order to:
John Muir Publications
P.O. Box 613
Santa Fe, NM 87504

Subtotal	$
Shipping	$1.50
Total Enclosed	$